QUIET MOMENTS
WITH GOD

DEVOTIONAL

RACINE, WI

Quiet Moments with God
ISBN: 978-1-970103-86-1 - *Paperback*
ISBN: 978-1-970103-87-8 - *Hardcover*
ISBN: 978-1-970103-41-0 - *Ebook*
Copyright © 2022 by Honor Books

Cover design by Faille Schmitz.

INTRODUCTION

Quiet moments—for personal reflection, for fellowship with God—we all need them, and we need them on a daily basis.

As our world moves and swirls past us, it's tempting to put those quiet times aside and regard them as luxuries rather than necessities. But the truth is—moments of quiet tranquility are critical. They help us define our relationships, our priorities, our goals, and ourselves. Without them, we become slaves to our lifestyles rather than the masters of them.

We hope you will find that the devotionals in this book help make your quiet moments productive and inspiring. We have selected those that relate best to the typical challenges of everyday life. And we have made them short enough to fit easily into your special time with God yet long enough to provide a solid kick-off for your day. As you read, we hope that they will draw you closer to God.

PREPARE TO DARE

Trying something new can be frightening and may even be dangerous. That's why it's much smarter to take a calculated risk than a reckless plunge.

> Every prudent man acts out of knowledge. But a fool exposes his folly.
>
> PROVERBS 13:16

A calculated risk is what Charles Lindbergh took when he decided to fly across the Atlantic, alone, in a single-engine plane. Was Lindbergh fearful? He certainly might have been if he had never flown before or if he had known nothing about planes. If he hadn't trusted the builder of his plane or his mechanics, he also would have had a good reason to be anxious. And if he had decided to make the trip on a whim, without advance planning, he certainly would have been labeled foolish.

But none of those factors were true in Lindbergh's case. He was an experienced pilot and mechanic who personally spent months overseeing the construction of his plane. He participated in the planning of every detail of his historic flight. The end result was a safe trip, finished ahead of schedule with fuel to spare.[1]

To a great extent, "Lucky Lindy" made his own luck. Likewise, heroic spiritual moments are nearly always grounded in advance preparation. Moses grew up in Pharaoh's court, unknowingly being prepared for the day he would demand that Pharaoh let his people leave

Egypt. Daniel was a man of prayer years before the king issued a decree banning prayer. The violation landed Daniel in a lion's den, where his prayers of protection were answered.

David was part of Saul's royal court and married to Saul's daughter. This was part of his preparation for assuming the throne one day. The years he spent in the wilderness prepared him spiritually to trust God, and God alone, to preserve him, protect him, and help him rule an empire. Esther prepared herself for a year before she won the "contest" to be queen.

You may not see clearly what God's purpose is for your life, but you can trust in the fact that He is preparing you for it. He will not waste a moment of your life. So make every relationship and experience count today, knowing He is grooming you for future greatness!

Every experience God gives us, every person he puts in our lives, is the perfect preparation for the future that only he can see.

CORRIE TEN BOOM

WHAT SHAPE ARE YOU IN?

Clay pots of all shapes and sizes were valuable tools in ancient households. Large jars were used to store water and olive oil; jugs were used to carry water; and small terra-cotta vials held perfume. Clay storage jars were filled with grain and other foods. Homemakers used clay pots for cooking. At mealtime, shallow pottery bowls were used as platters and dishes. In the evening the homes were lit by clay lamps.

The potters who supplied these much-needed pots were important to the economic life of ancient villages. A modern potter described her craft like this:

Both my hands shaped this pot. And, the place where it actually forms is a place of tension between the pressure applied from the outside and the pressure of the hand on the inside. That's the way my life has been. Sadness and death and misfortune and the love of friends and all the things that happened to me that I didn't even choose. All of that influenced my life. But, there are things I believe in about myself, my faith in God and the love of some friends that worked on the insides of me. My life, like this pot, is the result of what happened on the outside and what was going on inside of me. Life, like this pot, comes to be in places of tension.[2]

Throughout the day we may be buffeted by stress, pulled apart by responsibilities, and pressed by challenges that come at us from the outside. Without strength of spirit on the inside, those difficulties will cause us to collapse under the external pressure.

During this break, feed your spirit with Scripture. This will keep you strong, renewed, and restored within. You can respond with inner strength and creativity to what could otherwise defeat you.

Remember, your inner life gives you the strength you need to become a useful vessel in the household of God.

Renew thyself completely each day; do it
again, and again, and forever again.

CONFUCIUS

HOLD ON!

A little girl was very nervous at the prospect of her first horseback ride, even though she was to be perched behind her grandfather, who was an excellent rider. As her parents helped her onto the horse, she cried, "What do I do? I don't know how to ride a horse! I haven't done this before! What do I do?"

Her grandfather said in a reassuring tone, "Don't worry about the horse or about how to ride it. Just hold on to me, Darlin', just hold on to me."

> Preserve me, O God, for in you I put my trust.
>
> PSALM 16:1 NKJV

What good advice for us today! We thought our day was going to be a "tired-old-nag" sort of day, but it turned out to be a "bucking-bronco" day instead. On days like that, we need to "just hold on" to our faith in the Lord and stay in the saddle.

One of the foremost ways in which we hold on to the Lord is through constant communication with Him—a continual flow of prayer and praise. We can pray in any place at any time. Even a "thought" prayer turns our will and focus toward the Lord and puts our trust in Him. It is when we lose touch with the Lord that we are in danger of "falling" into panic and the frustration, frenzy, and failure that can come with it.

The Lord knows the end from the beginning of each day, and He knows how long the current upheaval in your life will last. Above all, He knows how to bring you safely through each "wild ride," keeping you in His divine peace all the way.

Harriet Beecher Stowe offered this advice:

When you get in a tight place and everything goes against you, till it seems you could not hold on a minute longer, never give up then, for that is just the place and time that the tide will turn.

Always remember that you don't "ride" the beasts of this life alone. The Lord is with you, and He has the reins firmly in His grasp. Just hold on!

Whatever God calls us to do, he also makes possible for us to accomplish.

UNKNOWN

ENERGY CRISIS

Most of us have a daily routine—a series of repetitious chores, errands, and tasks that demand our time and are required to maintain life at its most basic level. "Routine," says Jewish theologian Abraham Heschel, "makes us resistant to wonder." When we let our sense of wonder and awe drain away, we lose the sense of our preciousness to God.

> The joy of the Lord is your strength.
>
> NEHEMIAH 8:10 KJV

Jesus recognized our preoccupation with these duties in His Sermon on the Mount. He said, "Do not worry about your life, what you will eat or drink; or about your body, what you will wear. Is not life more important than food, and the body more important than clothes?" (Matthew 6:25).

But how do we apprehend the life that is "more important than food" when so much of our time and energy are spent providing and maintaining the essentials of food, clothing, and shelter? The "daily grind" can cause us to lose our sense of God's purpose and presence. We may feel like Job, who despaired, "When he passes me, I cannot see him; when he goes by, I cannot perceive him" (Job 9:11).

Julian of Norwich, the fourteenth-century English mystic, had a perspective that can help restore joy to even the most lackluster days. She said, "Joy is to see God in everything." The psalmist wrote, "The heavens declare the glory of God" (Psalm 19:1 KJV), and the prophet Isaiah wrote, "The whole earth is full of his glory" (Isaiah 6:3 KJV). The glory of creation is that it points us to the greater glory of the Creator.

If life's routines are wearing down your enthusiasm and joy, take time to seek out His love, majesty, and goodness revealed in creation. Be renewed in your joy of who God is—and who you are to Him—and find His strength and purpose in even your most routine tasks.

———————————

People need joy quite as much as clothing.
Some of them need it far more.

UNKNOWN

EASY AS A,B,C

"We need to run some tests." Those are words you never want to hear from a doctor. Our first inclination is to expect the worst.

Especially intimidating are the machines used to diagnose our disorders. The Magnetic Resonance Imager (MRI), with its oh-so-narrow magnetic metal tunnel, can bring out the claustrophobia in all of us.

A test like this causes a real break in our daily routine. (Have you noticed that most of them are scheduled in the morning?) While we might never reach the point where we look forward to such "breaks," we can do what one woman did to use the time constructively.

> In the day of trouble he will will keep me safe in his dwelling; he will hide me in the shelter of his tabernacle and set me high upon a rock.
>
> PSALM 27:5

Once inside the tube, she found herself on the verge of panic. Then she remembered some advice her pastor had given her: "When things are going badly for you, pray for someone else."

To simplify things, she decided to pray alphabetically. Several friends whose names began with A immediately came to mind. She prayed for Albert's sore knee, Amy's decision about work, and Andrew's upcoming final exams. She moved on to B and continued through the alphabet. By the letter D she was totally oblivious to her environment.

Thirty minutes later, she was only halfway through the alphabet, and the test was done. A day later, she used a short "break" in her doctor's office to complete her prayers while she waited for the test results, which showed no abnormalities.

Not all breaks are of our own design. Some are forced upon us and seem very unpleasant. But what we do with them is up to us.

When you find yourself taking a break that would not be your chosen activity, turn it over to your Father God and watch Him transform it into a special time for the two of you.

Faith is the capacity to trust God while
not being able to make sense out of
everything.

UNKNOWN

BALM

In centuries past, groves of balsam trees were planted on terraces in the hills south of Jerusalem. They were also planted in fields east of the Jordan River, in the area known as Gilead. The sap from the trees was harvested to create a balm that was considered to have great medicinal value in helping wounds to heal. The balm was used especially to treat scorpion stings and snake bites. Since scorpions and snakes abounded in the wilderness regions of Judea and throughout the Middle East, the balm was extremely valuable and was an important export item along ancient trade routes.[3]

> Is there no balm in Gilead, is there no physician there?
>
> JEREMIAH 8:22
> NKJV

The "balm of Gilead" is identified with Jesus. He is the One who heals our wounds.

Every day holds the potential for us to experience stings and bites, both literal and figurative. While not always life-threatening, these "jabs" from the enemy are hurtful nonetheless. How can we apply the balm of Jesus Christ to them?

The foremost way is through praise. Any time we find ourselves under attack or wounded, we can turn our minds and hearts to Him with a word, a thought, or a song of praise.

For example, if we feel attacked by a swarm of stinging problems, we can say, "Praise You, Jesus, You are my Deliverer, my Rescuer, my sure Help." If we feel wounded by a failure, we can say, "Praise You, Jesus, You are my Redeemer."

If we feel wounded in the heart by a word of criticism or rejection, we can say, "Praise You, Jesus, You have sent the Holy Spirit to be my Comforter." If we feel overwhelmed by too many responsibilities, we can say, "Praise You, Jesus, You are my Prince of Peace."

As you praise Jesus, you will find the pain associated with an incident or situation soothed. He is the Lord of Lords—including anything that tries to "lord" it over you!

We increase whatever we praise. The
whole creation responds to praise, and is
glad.

UNKNOWN

HOLY HUMOR

Is laughter theologically correct? We rarely think of a knee-slapping, rib-tickling, belly laugh when we think of being spiritual. But is that God's perspective?

> He who sits in the heavens shall laugh.
>
> PSALM 2:4 NKJV

In Umberto Eco's novel The Name of the Rose, a villainous monk named Jorge poisoned anyone who came upon the one book in the monastery library that suggested that God laughed. Jorge feared if the monks thought God laughed, God would become too familiar to them, too common, and they would lose their awe of Him. Jorge probably never considered the idea that laughter is one of the things that sets us apart as made in God's image.

In Spiritual Fitness, Doris Donnelly tells us that humor has two elements: an acceptance of life's incongruities and the ability not to take ourselves too seriously. The Christian faith is filled with incongruities—the meek inherit the earth, the simple teach wisdom, death leads to life, a virgin gives birth, a King is born in a stable. And many of life's incongruities are humorous.[4]

Humor also helps us let go of an exaggerated sense of importance to face the truth about ourselves. Anxiety over our own efforts can obscure what God is doing in our lives. "Lighten up" can be good spiritual advice!

How can we renew our sense of humor?

• Be on the lookout for humor. Almost every situation contains some element of humor.

• Spend time with people who have a sense of humor — their perspective will be contagious.

• Practice laughing. Take a five to ten-minute laugh break every day.

You can benefit from laughing. Humor requires a sense of honesty about yourself — without arrogance or false humility. Humor has also been proven to be good for your health. Take time to laugh each day — it is good for the soul as well as the body.

Laughter is an inexpensive way to
improve your health.

UNKNOWN

ENCUMBRANCES

In Jules Verne's novel *The Mysterious Island*, he writes of five men who escape a Civil War prison camp by hijacking a hot-air balloon. As they rise into the air, they realize the wind is carrying them over the ocean. Watching their homeland disappear on the horizon, they wonder how much longer the balloon will stay aloft.

As the hours pass and the surface of the ocean draws closer, the men decide they must cast some of the weight overboard because they have no way to heat the air in the balloon. Shoes, overcoats, and weapons are reluctantly discarded, and the uncomfortable aviators feel their balloon rise.

> Let us lay aside every weight, and the sin which so easily ensnares us.
>
> HEBREWS 12:1
> NKJV

However, it isn't long before they find themselves dangerously close to the waves again, so they toss their food overboard. Unfortunately, this, too, is only a temporary solution, and the craft again threatens to lower the men into the sea. One man has an idea: they can tie the ropes that hold the passenger car and sit on them. Then they can cut away the basket beneath them. As they do this, the balloon rises again.

Not a minute too soon, they spot land. The five jump into the water and swim to the island. They are alive because they were able to discern the difference between what was really needed and what was not. The "necessities" they once thought they couldn't live without were the very weights that almost cost them their lives.

Why not make an honest assessment of the things that might be slowing you down today? Are they physical or spiritual necessities for you or someone you love? What would your life be like without them? If you eliminated them, would you have more time for the things in your life that really matter?

Ask God to show you how your life could be improved if you made some changes and dropped some things that are weighing you down.

It's not enough to be busy . . . the question is: what are we busy about?

HENRY DAVID THOREAU

STOP AND THINK

God . . . richly furnishes us with everything to enjoy.

1 TIMOTHY 6:17 RSV

It seems that when you're in a hurry and running late, you hit nothing but red lights. Although they are annoying when we're racing to an appointment, stoplights are there for our protection.

We need stoplights throughout our day too. Hard work and busy schedules need to be interrupted with time for leisure and reflection. Without it we can become seriously sick with stress-induced illnesses. Time set aside for recreation or relaxation can rejuvenate our spirits. This poem by W. H. Davies tells us to take time to "stop and stare":

> What is this life if, full of care,
> We have no time to stand and stare.
> No time to stand beneath the boughs
> And stare as long as sheep or cows.
> No time to see, when woods we pass,
> Where squirrels hide their nuts in grass.
> No time to see, in broad daylight,
> Streams full of stars, like stars at night.
> No time to turn at Beauty's glance,
> And watch her feet, how they can dance.
> No time to wait till her mouth can
> Enrich that smile her eyes began.
> A poor life this if, full of care,
> We have no time to stand and stare.[5]

There are two ways of making it through our busy life. One way is to stop thinking. The second is to stop and think. Many people live the first way. They fill every hour with incessant activity. They dare not be alone. There is no time of quiet reflection in their lives. The second way, to stop and think, is to contemplate what life is for and to what end we are living. The word Sabbath literally means, "stop doing what you are doing."

Throughout the day today, give yourself a five- or ten-minute "mini-vacation." Get alone, be quiet, and listen for God to speak to you. Make time to be alone with God.

A happy life consists of tranquility of mind.

MARCUS TULLIUS CICERO

GOD'S PROMISE

A person who conducted an informal survey about the prayers of people in his church found that most people pray one of two types of prayers. The first was an SOS—not only "Save Our Souls," but also "Oh God, help us now."

The second was SOP—"Solve our Problems." People asked the Lord to eliminate all needs, struggles, trials, and temptations. They wanted carefree, perfect lives, and they fully believed that is what God had promised them. He concluded from his survey: "Most people want God to do it all."

God has not promised, however, to live our lives for us— but rather, to walk through our lives with us. Our part is to be faithful and obedient; His part is to lead us, guide us, protect us, and help us. Annie Johnson Flint recognized the true nature of God's promise in this poem:

I am with you all the days (perpetually, uniformly, and on very occasion), to the (very) close and consummation of the age.

MATTHEW 28:20 AMP

24

WHAT GOD HATH PROMISED

God hath not promised
Skies always blue,
Flower-strewn pathways
All our lives through;
God hath not promised
Sun without rain,
Joy without sorrow,
Peace without pain.
But God hath promised
Strength for the day,
Rest for the labor,
Light for the way,
Grace for the trials,
Help from above,
Unfailing sympathy,
Undying love.[6]

Do what you know you can do today—and then trust God to do what you cannot do!

You cannot control the length of your life, but you can control its width and depth.

EVAN ESAR

KNOWING YOUR WORTH

Let your yea be
yea; and your
nay, nay; lest
ye fall into
condemnation.

JAMES 5:12 KJV

In his book *Up from Slavery*, Booker T. Washington describes an ex-slave from Virginia:

I found that this man had made a contract with his master, two or three years previous to the Emancipation Proclamation, to the effect that the slave was to be permitted to buy himself, by paying so much per year for his body; and while he was paying for himself, he was to be permitted to labor where and for whom he pleased.

Finding that he could secure better wages in Ohio, he went there. When freedom came, he was still in debt to his master some 300 dollars. Notwithstanding that the Emancipation Proclamation freed him from any obligation to his master, this black man walked the greater portion of the distance back to where his old master lived in Virginia, and placed the last dollar, with interest, in his hands.

In talking to me about this, the man told me that he knew that he did not have to pay his debt, but that he had given his word to his master, and his word he had never broken. He felt that he could not enjoy his freedom till he had fulfilled his promise.[7]

Although he was born into slavery, the man Washington described obviously knew his worth. More important, he knew that as a free child of God, his word should be trustworthy. He knew he would sleep peacefully if he kept his word to others.

We live in a world where giving our word is not taken seriously. God wants us to walk in blessing and sleep in peace, and that's why He exhorts us to stand by our word.

Be aware of all the times you make promises to people today, and make sure you follow through. Not only will you sleep more peacefully, but your friends, family, neighbors, and coworkers will have a new respect for you as well.

Self-respect is the noblest garment with
which a man may clothe himself.

SAMUEL SMILES

WAYSIDE STOPS

A sanctuary is a place of refuge and protection—a place where you can leave the world behind.

Travelers in the Middle Ages found little shrines set up along the roadway. In each shrine, a cross and the image of a saint were hung. Travelers could stop at these "sanctuaries" for rest and prayer, regaining strength to continue their journey.

Our contemporary world doesn't have wayside shrines for rest stops. But our minds and hearts still get weary. We have to devise our own wayside stops, not on actual roads, but in the road of daily life.

> Jesus . . . withdrew again to a mountain by himself.
>
> JOHN 6:15

Attending a worship service on a weekend does not usually provide everything we need to see us through an entire week. As inspiring as the service may be, we need something more to keep us going until the next service. We need stopping places during the week, intimate sanctuaries here and there where we can stop and let God refresh our soul with His presence.

What are some sanctuaries you might find to get away and find restoration?

• Reading Scripture is one such stopping place.

Immerse yourself in a favorite passage or Psalm.

• A little book of devotion—such as the one you are reading now—is a good way to restore energy.

• A trusted Christian friend with whom you can be yourself is a type of sanctuary. You can gain a great deal from the faith, encouragement, and insight of others.

• Your own communion service during the week gives you a chance to take part in the nourishment of the Lord's Supper.

• Going to a park or sitting in your own backyard and reading gives you a chance to rest while enjoying God's creation.

• Singing aloud a great hymn or praise song helps to restore your joy.

Jesus is your Example, and He often went away to a quiet place to gain strength from His Heavenly Father. Establish your own personal shrines today!

What sweet delight a quiet life affords.

WILLIAM HAWTHORDEN
DRUMMOND

WHAT DO YOU KNOW?

"Knowledge is of two kinds," said Samuel Johnson. "We know a subject ourselves, or we know where we can find information upon it."

There's also a third area of knowledge: the unknowable. Try as we might to uncover all the secrets of the universe, there are simply some things we will never discover or comprehend. As the Apostle Paul told the Corinthians, "Now I know in part; then [in the afterlife] I shall know fully, even as I am fully known" (1 Corinthians 13:12).

It's tempting to become a know-it-all. Knowing how to do something, how to fix something, or how to find something gives us a good feeling. We have all experienced the rewards associated with learning new skills and developing them to the best of our ability.

Most of us also enjoy having others turn to us for answers or information. Much of our self-esteem is derived from what we know and what we can do.

> I consider everything a loss compared to the surpassing greatness of knowing Christ Jesus my Lord.
>
> PHILIPPIANS 3:8

But there must be a balance. We must face the hard fact that we can never know everything there is to know about anything. We can never achieve perfection of skill to the point where we never make mistakes. In fact, the more we know about something, the more we realize how much we don't know. The more proficient our skills, the more we are aware that accidents happen, some days are "off" days, and everyone has a slump now and then.

If we choose, we can become obsessed with our own perfection and potential, spending all our available time reading, studying, and taking courses. We might listen to teaching tapes while we jog and make every vacation "a learning experience."

A wiser approach to life, however, is to spend more time knowing God. The more you know Him, the easier it is to trust Him; hear His voice; and show His love to your family, friends, neighbors, and coworkers. You will learn the things you will need to know in order to do His will. What we know and can do is never as satisfying or meaningful as knowing God and serving others.

Instead of trying to become a bank of information, become a channel of blessing!

Teach me, my God and King, in all things
thee to see; and what I do in anything, to
do it as for thee!

GEORGE HERBERT

SHORTSIGHTED

Do you miss life-changing opportunities because of shortsightedness? Consider this example:

> As we have therefore opportunity, let us do good unto all men, especially unto them who are of the household of faith.
>
> GALATIANS 6:10 KJV

A fellow approached a cab driver in New York and said, "Take me to London." The cab driver told him there was no possible way for him to drive across the Atlantic. The customer insisted there was. "You'll drive me down to the pier; we'll put the taxi on a freighter to Liverpool; and you'll drive me to London, where I'll pay you whatever is on the meter."

The driver agreed, and when they arrived in London, the passenger paid the total on the meter, plus a thousand dollar tip.

The driver roamed around London, not quite knowing what to do. Then an Englishman hailed him and said, "I want you to drive me to New York." The cab driver couldn't believe his good luck. How often can you pick up a person in London who wants to go to New York?

When the passenger began to say, "First, we take a boat . . ." the driver cut him off.

"That I know. But where to in New York?"

The passenger said, "Riverside Drive and 104th Street."

The driver responded, "Sorry, I don't go to the west side."

Jesus was well schooled in the Scriptures, and He often followed the traditions of His heritage. He also had a daily routine of praying and ministering to the needs of the people. However, He didn't allow traditions or personal preferences to stand in the way of carrying out God's will for the day.

Look for God-given opportunities to serve Him by serving others. Don't allow your daily routines, personal biases, or shortsightedness cause you to miss what the Lord wants to do in you and through you today.

A good deed is never lost: he who shows
courtesy reaps friendship, and he who
plants kindness gathers love.

SAINT BASIL

GOD IS GOOD

An ancient legend of a swan and a crane tells us about God's goodness—which may be different from what we believe to be good.

A beautiful swan came to rest by the banks of a pond where a crane was wading, seeking snails. For a few minutes the crane looked at the swan and then asked, "Where do you come from?"

The swan replied, "I come from Heaven!"

"And where is Heaven?" asked the crane.

> Friend, go up higher.
>
> LUKE 14:10 KJV

"Heaven!" replied the swan, "Heaven! Have you never heard of Heaven?" And the beautiful swan went on to describe the splendor and grandeur of the eternal city. She told the crane about the streets of gold and the gates and walls made of precious stones. She told about the river of life which was as pure as crystal. On the banks of this river stood a tree with leaves for the healing of the nations of the world. In great and eloquent language, the swan described the hosts of saints and angels who lived in the world beyond.

Somewhat surprisingly, the crane didn't appear to be the least bit interested in this place the swan described. Eventually he asked the swan, "Are there any snails there?"

"Snails!" declared the swan, obviously revolted at

the thought. "No! Of course there are not!"

"Then you can have your Heaven," said the crane, as it continued its search along the slimy, muddy banks of the pond. "What I want is snails!"[8]

This fable has a profound truth in it. How many of us turn our backs on the good God has for us in order to search for snails?

Seek out the good that God has for you today. Ask God to give you the desire for His good, instead of what you consider to be good. Don't bury your head deep in slime when God wants you to experience the delights and joy of His Heaven!

———————————

Our love for God is tested by the question
of whether we seek him or his gifts.

RALPH WASHINGTON SOCKMAN

FORM AND SUBSTANCE

America's preoccupation with "image" seems to have reached outrageous proportions. Christians, like everyone else, want to put their best feet forward as often as possible. Unfortunately, this can sometimes lead to majoring on form and nearly losing substance altogether. Consider this story:

A devout Christian who had a cat used to spend several minutes each day at prayer and meditation in his bedroom. He read a portion of Scripture and a devotional book, followed by a period of silent meditation and prayer. As time went on, his prayers became longer and more intense. He came to cherish this quiet time in his bedroom, but his cat came to like it too. She would cozy up to him, purr loudly, and rub her furry body against him. This interrupted the man's prayer time, so he put a collar around the cat's neck and tied her to the bedpost whenever he wanted to be undisturbed while at prayer. This didn't seem to upset the cat, and it meant the man could meditate without interruption.

> When you pray, go into your room, close the door and pray to your Father, who is unseen. Then your Father, who sees what is done in secret, will reward you.
>
> MATTHEW 6:6

Over the years, the daughter of this devout Christian had noted how much his devotional time had meant to him. When she began to establish some routines and patterns for her own family, she decided she should do as her father had done. Dutifully, she tied her cat to the bedpost and then proceeded with her devotions. But in her generation, time moved faster, and she couldn't spend as much time at prayer as her father did.

The day came when her son was grown up. He also wanted to preserve some of the family tradition that had meant so much to his mother and his grandfather. But the pace of life had quickened all the more, and there simply was no time for elaborate devotional proceedings. So he eliminated the time for meditation, Bible reading, and prayer. But in order to carry on the tradition, each day while he was dressing, he tied the family cat to the bedpost!

He who ceases to pray ceases to prosper.

SIR WILLIAM GURNEY BENHAM

WINDOW ON
THE WORLD

A story from England called "The Wonderful Window" tells about a London clerk who worked in drab and depressing circumstances. His office building was in a rundown part of the city and had not been maintained.

> O Lord, I Pray, open his eyes that he may see.
>
> 2 KINGS 6:17
> NASB

But that ordinary clerk was not about to let his outlook on life be determined by the dreariness of his surroundings. So one day he bought a beautiful, multicolored Oriental window painted with an inspiring scene.

The clerk took his window to his workplace and had it installed high up on the wall in his office. When the hardworking, dispirited clerk looked through his window, he did not see the familiar slum scenes, with dark streets and dirty marketplaces. Instead he saw a fair city with beautiful castles and towers, green parks, and lovely homes on wide tree-lined streets. On the highest tower of the window there was a large white banner with a strong knight protecting the fair city from a fierce and dangerous dragon. This wonderful window put a "halo" on the everyday tasks of the young man.

Somehow as he worked long hours at tedious book work and accounting, trying to make everything balance, he felt he was working for that knight on the banner. This feeling produced a sense of honor and dignity. He had found a noble purpose helping the knight keep the city happy, beautiful, prosperous, and strong.

You don't have to let your circumstances or surroundings discourage you, either. God has sent you to your place of work—whether it is at home, in an office, at a school, or in a factory—to do noble work for Him. You are His worker, bringing His beauty to everyone around you.

———————————————

It is our best work that God wants, not the dregs of our exhaustion. I think he must prefer quality over quantity.

GEORGE MACDONALD

THE TROUBLE BEING RIGHT

Believe it or not, it's often harder to gracefully receive an apology than it is to issue one. As Christians, we know we are to forgive "seventy times seven" times (Matthew 18:22 KJV), but some of us can sincerely forgive and still project an air of superiority unbecoming to a child of the King.

> Take heed to yourselves: if thy brother trespass against thee, rebuke him; and if he repent, forgive him.
>
> LUKE 17:3 KJV

If you're waiting for someone to realize they owe you an apology, use your coffee break to think of a response that reflects genuine forgiveness and allows the transgressor to feel he or she has retained your respect. Consider this humorous little story:

A passenger on a dining car looked over the luncheon menu. The list included both a chicken salad sandwich and a chicken sandwich. He decided on the chicken salad sandwich but absent-mindedly wrote chicken sandwich on the order slip. When the waiter brought the chicken sandwich, the customer angrily protested.

Most waiters would have immediately picked up the order slip and shown the customer the mistake was his. This waiter didn't. Instead, expressing regret at the error, he picked up the chicken sandwich, returned to the kitchen, and a moment later placed a chicken salad sandwich in front of the customer.

While eating his sandwich, the customer picked up the order slip and saw that the mistake was his. When it came time to pay the check, the man apologized to the waiter and offered to pay for both sandwiches. The waiter's response was, "No, sir. That's perfectly all right. I'm just happy you've forgiven me for being right."

By taking the blame initially and allowing the passenger to discover his own mistake, the waiter accomplished several things: he allowed the passenger to retain his dignity, reminded him to be more cautious before blaming others, and created a better atmosphere for everyone in the dining car. Next time people blame you for their mistakes, don't get defensive, but instead find a creative way to make things right.

It is not who is right, but what is right,
that is of importance.

THOMAS HUXLEY

PRAYER PAUSE

A coffee break is a good time for prayer!

When we pray at the outset of our day, our prayer is often for general guidance and help from the Lord. When we pray in the midst of our day, our prayer is much more likely to be specific and aimed at immediate needs and concerns. By the time a coffee break rolls around, we have a much better idea of what our day holds, including what particular dangers, difficulties, or temptations we are going to face! It is with that knowledge, born of experience, that this prayer of Saint Patrick takes on even greater meaning:

> *May the wisdom of God instruct me,*
> *the eye of God watch over me,*
> *the ear of God hear me,*
> *the word of God give me sweet talk,*
> *the hand of God defend me,*
> *the way of God guide me.*
> *Christ be with me.*
> *Christ before me.*
> *Christ in me.*
> *Christ under me.*
> *Christ over me.*
> *Christ on my right hand.*
> *Christ on my left hand.*
> *Christ on this side.*
> *Christ on that side.*
> *Christ in the head of everyone to whom I speak.*
> *Christ in the mouth of every person who speaks to me.*
> *Christ in the eye of every person who looks upon me.*
> *Christ in the ear of everyone who hears me today.*

Amen.[9]

Take time in the middle of your day to ask the Lord for His wrap-around presence, His unending encouragement, and His all-sustaining assistance. And in return, be a vessel that carries His presence, encouragement, and assistance to others.

Uphold me according to your promise,

that I may live.

PSALM 119:116 AMP

Do not look upon the vessel, but upon

what it holds.

HEBREW PROVERB

GOD KNOWS!

Do you ever wonder if God has lost your address? Do you ever think perhaps He has lost track of you or even forgotten you altogether? God's Word answers those thoughts with a resounding, "Not so!"

> Even the very hairs of your head are all numbered.
>
> MATTHEW 10:30 AMP

Jesus taught His followers, "Are not two little sparrows sold for a penny? And yet not one of them will fall to the ground without your Father's leave (consent) and notice . . . Fear not, then; you are of more value than many sparrows" (Matthew 10:29,31 AMP).

The psalmist also recognized God's thorough and intimate knowledge of us. Read these words from Psalm 139, and be encouraged. The Lord not only knows you, but He knows precisely what you are facing and experiencing today. Even if you are not aware of His presence, you can rest assured He is by your side:

O Lord, you have examined my heart and know everything about me. You know when I sit or stand. When far away you know my every thought. You chart the path ahead of me, and tell me where to stop and rest. Every moment, you know where I am. You know what I am going to say before I even say it. You both precede and follow me, and place your hand of blessing on my head.

This is too glorious, too wonderful . . . I can never be

lost to your Spirit! I can never get away from my God!

You saw me before I was born and scheduled each day of my life before I began to breathe. Every day was recorded in your Book!

———————————————————————

How precious it is, Lord, to realize that
you are thinking about me constantly! I
can't even count how many times a day
your thoughts turn towards me. And
when I awaken in the morning, you are
still thinking of me!

PSALMS 139:1-7,16-18 TLB

Before God created the universe, he
already had you in mind.

ERWIN W. LUTZER

WHOSE STRENGTH?

In the springtime it's fun to watch tiny baby birds with downy crowns begin to find their way around. They make their way to the edge of their nest and take a peek over to view the very large, unexplored world around them.

> When I am weak, then I am strong.
>
> 2 CORINTHIANS 12:10 NKJV

At first they may look into the abyss and then shrink back to the familiar security of their nest. Perhaps they imagine the strength of their own untried wings is all that will save them from a fatal fall—and they know how weak and unproven those little wings are! Yet, when they are either pushed out of the nest or gather courage to launch out on their own to try that first flight, they find the air supports them when they spread their wings.

How often do we allow unfamiliar situations and circumstances to loom large and threatening in our imagination? Sometimes when we look at circumstances that lie outside our familiar "nest" we may feel just like a baby bird. We take a look at our own weakness, and we may want to turn around and head back to safety.

In times of crisis—either real or imagined—what is it that God has called us to do? He may be trying to push us out of our nest and "stretch our wings," so we can grow in our faith.

When Peter saw the Lord Jesus walking on the Sea of Galilee, he cried out, "Lord, if it's you, tell me to come to you on the water." Jesus replied, "Come." Peter got out of the boat and walked on the water toward Jesus. It was when he took his eyes off Jesus and focused on the wind, that he became frightened and began to sink. He cried out, "Lord, save me!" And, of course, Jesus did! (See Matthew 14:27-31.)

When you look to your own resources, you may get a "sinking" feeling. This morning, look to Jesus and His resources. Then you will have courage to venture into unknown territory!

Let us not pray for lighter burdens, but
for stronger backs.

AMISH SAYING

KNOWING GOD'S WILL

Knowing the will of God—both the big picture and the daily details—concerns every Christian. We all need to ask often, *What is it God wants me to do? How is it He wants me to live?*

Saint Ignatius of Loyola saw the doing of God's will as not only our command in life, but also our reward:

Teach us, good Lord, to serve thee as thou deservest: to give and not to count the cost; to fight and not to heed the wounds; to toil and not to seek for rest; to labor and not to ask for any reward save that of knowing that we do thy will.[10]

> I pray you, if I have found favor in your sight, show me now your way.
>
> EXODUS 33:13 AMP

It is as we know we are doing God's will that we find true meaning in life and a deep sense of accomplishment and purpose.

How can we know that we are doing God's will? One of the simplest approaches is this:

• Commit yourself to the Lord each day, and periodically throughout the day, by simply saying, "Lord, I put my life in Your hands. Do with me what You will."

• Trust the Lord to send you the work and the relationships you need for His purpose in your life to be accomplished.

As Roberta Hromas, a noted Bible teacher, once said: "Simply answer your door, answer your phone, and answer your mail. The Lord will put in your path the opportunities that He desires for you to pursue."

God's will is not a mystery you try desperately to unlock. He does not desire His will to be a secret because the Bible is filled with scriptures about knowing His will. The key is to seek His will, to listen to the Holy Spirit, and to read and study His Word. Then you can know what He has planned for you!

A man's heart is right when he wills what God wills.

SAINT THOMAS AQUINAS

THE RIPPLE EFFECT

Not all people who commit their lives to Jesus Christ will be called to be world famous. The majority of us are called to fulfill less noticeable roles in our churches, communities, and families. Yet only God may know how significant our roles are to the future of thousands—even millions.

A century and a half ago a humble minister lived and died in a small village in Leicestershire, England. He lived there his entire life and never traveled far from home. He never attended college and had no formal degrees, but he was a faithful village minister.

In his congregation was a young cobbler to whom he gave special attention, teaching him the Word of God. This young man was William Carey, later hailed as one of the greatest missionaries of modern times.

The village minister also had a son—a boy whom he taught faithfully and encouraged constantly. The boy's character and talents were profoundly impacted by his father's life. That son grew up to be a man many considered the mightiest public orator of his day: Robert Hall. Widely admired for his saintly character, his

The mustard seed indeed is the least of all seeds; but when it is grown, it is the greatest among herbs, and becometh a tree, so that the birds of the air come and ledge I the branches thereof.

MATTHEW 13:32 KJV

preaching was powerful, and his sermons influenced the decisions of statesmen.

It seems the village pastor accomplished little in his life as a preacher. There were no spectacular revivals, great miracles, or major church growth. But his faithful witness and Godly life had much to do with giving India its Carey and England its Robert Hall.

When you think you are having no impact in the world by teaching a Sunday school class or visiting those who are homebound, remember the little country preacher who influenced two nations for the Lord.

We never know what ripple of healing we set in motion by simply smiling on one another.

HENRY DRUMMOND

IN PROGRESS

A sign in a hotel lobby that was being remodeled stated, "Please be patient. Renovation in progress to produce something new and wonderful." Perhaps we all need to wear a sign like that! We are all unfinished projects under construction, being made into something wonderful. Being mindful of this, we might have greater grace and patience for others, as well as for ourselves, while the work is underway.

> He who has began a good work in your will complete it until the day of Jesus Christ.
>
> PHILIPPIANS 1:6 NKJV

Hope is the anticipation of good. Like the hotel lobby in the disarray of renovation, our hope is often in spite of our present circumstances. What is the basis for our hope?

For the Christian, hope is not simple optimism or a denial of reality. The Reason for our hope is Jesus Christ, the solid Rock of our faith. As the hymn writer wrote, "My hope is built on nothing less than Jesus' blood and righteousness." We are never without hope for our lives if we know the Lord Jesus.

The focus of our hope is to be like Jesus. This goal may seem too great and way beyond our ability to achieve, and it is. So how do we reach it?

The Scriptures tell us it is "Christ in you" that is our hope. (See Colossians 1:27.) The transformation of our lives into Christlikeness is a goal that is larger than life.

As Paul wrote to the Corinthians, to have hope only for this life is to be miserable. (See 1 Corinthians 15:19.) The Christian hope is for this life and for eternity.

A little chapel in the hills of the Scottish Highlands has a sign chiseled in Gaelic on the front door. Translated into English it reads: "Come as you are, but don't leave as you came." When we come to Jesus, we can come as we are. But He will not leave us the same. That is our sure hope.[11]

Our hope lies, not in the man we put on the moon, but in the man we put on the cross.

DON BASHAM

DO-IT-YOURSELF MISERY

> Deceit is in the heart of them that imagine evil; but to the counsellors of peace is joy.
>
> PROVERBS 12:20 KJV

Some people just can't figure out why life has dealt them such a miserable hand. They see others around them enjoying life, and that only adds to their misery. They're convinced their horrible lot in this world is a plot by others to keep them down. In truth, misery is always self-concocted. Here's a sure-fire recipe for misery printed in the Gospel Herald:

- Think about yourself.
- Talk about yourself.
- Use "I" as often as possible.
- Mirror yourself continually in the opinion of others.
- Listen greedily to what people say about you.
- Be suspicious.
- Expect to be appreciated.
- Be jealous and envious.
- Be sensitive to slights.
- Never forgive a criticism.
- Trust nobody but yourself.
- Insist on consideration and the proper respect.
- Demand agreement with your own views on everything.
- Sulk if people are not grateful to you for favors

shown them.
- Never forget a service you may have rendered.
- Be on the lookout for a good time for yourself.
- Shirk your duties if you can.
- Do as little as possible for others.
- Love yourself supremely.
- Be selfish.[12]

This recipe is guaranteed to work. In fact, you don't even need all the ingredients to achieve total misery.

On the other hand, if misery's not your idea of a good time, do just the opposite. If you do, you'll have a hard time feeling even a little blue!

For most men the world is centered in
self, which is misery; to have one's world
centered in God is peace.

DONALD HANKHY

A "BODY OF WORK"

Sixty-five years has within it exactly 569,400 hours. If you subtract the number of hours that a person spends growing up and receiving a basic high-school education, and then subtract the hours that a person normally spends eating, sleeping, and engaging in recreation, you will still have 134,000 hours for work between the ages of eighteen and sixty-five.

That's a lot of time! Yet, many people reach retirement age, look back over their years, and conclude: "I was only putting in time and drawing a paycheck."

Take a different approach, starting today. Choose to create a "body of work" with the time that you have!

> Christ Jesus . . . gave himself on our behalf that he might redeem us (purchase our freedom) from all iniquity and purify for himself a people (to be peculiarly his own).
>
> TITUS 2:13-14 AMP

A body of work is more than a career or a pile of achievements, awards, and accomplishments. A "body" of work is just that—physical and human. A body of work is people.

King David desired to build a great temple for the Lord. The prophet Nathan came to Him with God's Word on the idea: "The Lord declares to you that He will make for you a house." David had in mind mortar and cedar. The

Lord had in mind family and relationships! (See 2 Samuel 7.)

Get to know the people with whom you work. Spend time with them. Value them. Share experiences with them. Be there when they face crises and when they celebrate milestones. Count your colleagues — and also those above and below you on the organizational ladder — among your friends, and treat them as friends. Build relationships that endure through the years, regardless of who is transferred, promoted, or laid off. People are what will matter to you far more than possessions when you reach your retirement years.

See everything; overlook a great deal;

correct a little.

POPE JOHN XXIII

MAKE HAY WHILE
THE SUN SHINES

Medicine—what a glamorous profession! High salaries, prestige, respect, travel, speaking engagements, curing the sick, and discovering new drugs.

> This is what the Lord says: "Stand at the crossroads and look; ask for the ancient paths, ask where the good way is, and walk in it, and you will find rest for your souls."
>
> JEREMIAH 6:16

Medicine—occasional tedium, exposure to a host of diseases, making an incorrect diagnosis, watching patients die, long hours, no sleep, no family time, and malpractice suits.

Medicine—maybe not so glamorous after all.

When doctors spend most of the year trying to help their patients sort out various physical and mental ailments, while trying not to become emotionally involved, where do they go to heal their own wounded spirits?

One doctor in Michigan goes back home to Vermont to help her father and brother with the haying. "It's elegantly simple work," she says. The job has a set of basic steps which, when followed, result in neatly bound bales of hay that are then trucked off the fields and sold the following winter. Haying is hot, sweaty, tiring work, but it has a satisfying beginning, middle, and end . . . unlike medicine.[13]

All of us need an activity that is the antithesis of what we do all day. We need a cobweb-clearer, a routine-shaker.

Those who engage in mental work all day often find crafts or hobbies that involve their hands to be very rewarding and enjoyable. Conversely, those who engage in hard manual labor often enjoy working puzzles, reading, or engaging in a course of study.

Those who work with people in high-stress environments frequently find great pleasure in gardening or other solitary activities. Those who work alone often enjoy spending their off hours with other people.

We each need to be completely out of our normal work mode for a little while every day—and for a week or two when we can manage it. It's a crucial part of living a balanced life!

Take rest; a field that has rested gives a
bountiful crop.

OVID

DAILY BREAD

The Lord Jesus knows our need for physical and spiritual nourishment. He knows we can't make it on our own, that in depending on our own resources we don't have what it takes for everyday life — let alone for everlasting life. In fact, we were created to depend on Him.

When Jesus instituted the Last Supper, He told His disciples to "do this in remembrance of me" (Luke 22:19). Remembering someone is to allow them to shape and influence our lives. Jesus was asking His disciples to remember Him in the Lord's Supper so that even when He was no longer physically present with them, He would still be shaping and guiding their lives. When we go to the Lord's Table, we give witness to the fact we are depending upon Jesus.

As we remember Jesus, we have the picture of Him giving himself to us to nurture and feed our souls. A song written by Arden Autry describes how He lovingly gave — and continues to give — His life for us:

We do not have a high priest who cannot sympathize with our weaknesses, but was in all points tempted as we are, yet without sin.

HEBREWS 4:15 NKJV

As you eat this bread, as you drink this cup,
Let your heart give thanks and be lifted up.
Your soul can rest in this truth secure:
As you eat this bread, all I am is yours.

All I am is yours. All I am I gave,
Dying on the cross, rising from the grave,
Your sins to bear and your life restore:
As you eat this bread, all I am is yours.

In delight and joy, in the depths of pain,
In the anxious hours, through all loss and gain,
Your world may shake, but my Word endures:
As you eat this bread, all I am is yours.[14]

During this coffee break and throughout your day, remember Jesus. Let Him direct your thoughts and ways. It is His strength and wisdom that will give you success and fulfillment in life.

_____

The mind grows by what it feeds on.

JOSIAH GILBERT HOLLAND

MORNING BY MORNING

Great is Thy faithfulness,

Oh God my Father!

Morning by morning, new mercies I see.

All I have needed, Thy hands hath provided.

Great is Thy faithfulness, Lord, unto me.

TRADITIONAL HYMN

O God, thou art my God; early will I seek thee.

PSALM 63:1 KJV

There's something fresh and new about the beginning of each day. As sun filters through the trees, as birds begin their morning song, as day dawns, there is a new awareness of God's hand at work in our hearts and lives. Yesterday is past; tomorrow is still a day away. But today offers a new beginning—here and now.

In the morning, O Lord, you hear my voice; in the morning I lay my requests before you and wait in expectation.

PSALM 5:3

Throughout Scripture, the Lord invites us to spend time with Him before we face the demands of our lives. He urges us to seek Him first, to give our best to Him first, and to ask Him first.

Why? Because we need Him. And knowing that we need Him is always a good place to start any day.

Just as a good night's sleep refreshes the body, so a quiet moment with God at daybreak revitalizes our spirit before the day's responsibilities descend upon us. Starting the day with a holy hush before the morning rush can make the difference between a day wasted and a day well lived.

Rejoicing comes in the morning.
PSALM 30:5

No matter what happened yesterday, you have today. It is a gift from your Heavenly Father. Open your heart to a quiet moment with God. May these gentle, joyful devotionals help you celebrate your faith in God, renew your mind, refresh your spirit, and encourage your heart.

All the troubles of life come upon us
because we refuse to sit quietly for a while
each day in our rooms.

BLAISE PASCAL

HOLY HUSH

All is still as a man sits at his dining room table, allowing the pages of a well-worn Bible to slip slowly through his fingers and basking in the peace of the moment. The pages have a comfortable feel, and the soft plop they make as they fall barely disturbs the quiet. Early morning always brings with it a hush of holiness for him. In his mind's eye he remembers another such morning.

> You, O Lord, are a compassionate and gracious God, slow to anger and abounding in love and faithfulness.
>
> PSALM 86:15

The new dawn air is tangy and sharp as he and his brother turn onto a gravel road bordered by wheat fields. Early in the growing season the wheat is about two feet high and a brilliant green. Suddenly the boy catches his breath. From the edge of the wheat field, a ring-necked pheasant comes into view just as a bright ray of sunshine creates a natural spotlight. As if showing off for God himself, the pheasant stops and strikes a pose.

Time stands still, sound ceases, and God paints an image on the young boy's mind that will remain for a lifetime. The beautiful hues of the pheasant, with its shining white collar glistening in the sunshine against the vivid green of the wheat, remain sharply etched in his memory. Whenever he relives that day, he experiences anew the presence of God and a supernatural sense of contentment. Slowly the memory recedes, but the presence of God remains.

Sir Thomas Brown said, "Nature is the art of God." All around us are awesome reminders of a big God who created everything in a matter of days. Isn't it great to know the Artist firsthand?

When God makes his presence felt
through us, we are like the burning bush;
Moses never took any heed was sort of
bush it was - he only saw the brightness
of the Lord.

GEORGE ELIOT

WAKE-UP CALL

> Awake to righteousness and sin not.
>
> 1 CORINTHIANS 15:34 KJV

Boot camp was a rude awakening for a young man who entered the Army to get away from his parents' rules. He reasoned that going into the service would give him the freedom he wanted to do whatever he pleased. He knew boot camp would be tough, but he was certain he could handle it. Besides, boot camp only lasted for six weeks. After that he would be free!

Upon waking that first morning to his sergeant's yells, the young soldier came face to face with the reality that Mom, Dad, and all his teachers clumped together couldn't compare to what he was about to face. His six weeks loomed as an eternity. He regularly wrote his family and included the first thank-you notes his parents had ever received from their son. He even expressed thanks for what his teachers had done for him.

This young soldier found out quickly the importance of learning how to handle what could attack a soldier in war. He was faced with a reason to wake up and a reason to be prepared. The sergeant trained the young recruits to anticipate the enemy's strategy, making certain they knew the enemy was lurking and ready to attack without warning. He taught them that the enemy is extremely cunning and watches and waits to attack during their weakest, most vulnerable times.

The Bible tells us to awake to righteousness and to prepare ourselves, so we will not sin. God has provided the right armor and training required to defeat the enemy. We become soldiers for Christ when we join His family. God's enemies are our enemies, and the battle is over the most precious of God's creations: the human soul.

God shall be my hope, my stand, my

guide, and lantern to my feet.

WILLIAM SHAKESPEARE

GOOD MORNING, LORD

There is something extraordinarily special about early morning devotions. Before the hectic day begins with its noise and numerous distractions, there is usually a calm that is uncommon to any other time of the day, a peaceful prerequisite for entering into the prayer closet with Christ. Christ set an example for us when He rose up early and prayed.

Morning is the first step to the list of "things to do" written out the night before and to a world of unknown plans prepared by God for us to become acquainted with. Morning is a wonderfully private time where intimate conversation and gentle responses can take place between God and His children. This is a time to listen to the very heart of God.

Oswald Chambers said, "Get an inner chamber in which to pray where no one knows you are praying, shut the door, and talk to God in secret. Have no other motive than to know your Father in heaven. It is impossible to conduct your life as a disciple without definite times of secret prayer."

In the morning, O Lord, thou wilt hear my voice; in the morning I will order my prayer to thee and eagerly watch.

PSALM 5:3 NASB

Between Midnight and Morning
You that have faith to look with fearless eyes
Beyond the tragedy of a world of strife,
And trust that out of night and death shall rise
The dawn of ampler life;
Rejoice, whatever anguish rend your heart,
That God has given you, for a priceless dower,
To live in these great times and have your part
In Freedom's crowning hour;
That we may tell your sons who see the light
High in heaven — their heritage to take —
"I saw the powers of darkness put to flight!
I saw the morning break!"

OWEN SEAMAN

I can tell you that God is alive because I talked with him this morning.

BILLY GRAHAM

THE ART OF CARING

This was the first meeting of a support group for middle school youngsters who had suffered significant losses in their lives. The group leader was unsure of what to expect, so the question really caught him by surprise.

"Why does God kill babies?"

The question hung in the air for an eternity, and two young faces stared intently at the group counselor, waiting for an answer. He gazed at the two brothers' faces as he contemplated how to respond. He wished to reassure them that God does not kill babies, yet, for the moment, the answer to the question seemed far less important than what prompted it.

"Something really sad must have happened for you guys to ask such a question," he finally responded.

> Now these three remain: faith, hope, and love, but he greatest of these is love.
>
> 1 CORINTHIANS 13:13

The two brothers shared the sad story of how their entire family had hoped for a new baby. The boys wanted to become uncles in the worst way.

Finally, their older sister became pregnant, but the baby was stillborn. They could not understand why this would happen.

With careful encouragement and much listening, the

70

counselor found a way for the two brothers to come to grips with the loss of their niece. Although they eventually understood that the loss of their niece was not a direct act of God, they still struggled with why it happened.

As the other group members shared their own stories of loss and sadness, a kinship developed among the group that lifted the sadness. It seems that once people allow themselves to honestly share their sadness, then the darkness cannot remain.

Psychologist Rollo May said, "Care is a state in which something does matter; it is the source of human tenderness." Take time to care every chance you get!

The capacity to care gives life its deepest significance.

PABLO CASALS

JUST THE FACTS

There was once a man that John Wesley thought of as miserly; therefore, he had little respect for him. He felt so strongly about this man that, on an occasion when the man gave only a small gift to a worthy charity, Wesley openly criticized him.

> He that is void of wisdom despiseth his neighbor; but. a man of understanding holdeth his peace.
>
> PROVERBS 11:12 KJV

Not long after, the gentleman paid a visit to Wesley. He was surprised to hear that this man—someone whom he assumed was simply greedy—had actually been living on parsnips and water for several weeks. The man told him that, in his past, he had amassed a great deal of debt. But since his conversion, he had made a choice to pay off all of his creditors and, therefore, was buying nothing for himself and spending as little as possible elsewhere in order to do so.

"Christ has made me an honest man," he said, "and so with all these debts to pay, I can give only a few offerings above my tithe. I must settle up with my worldly neighbors and show them what the grace of God can do in the heart of a man who was once dishonest." Wesley then apologized to the man and asked his forgiveness.[15]

It's easy to find fault with others when we don't

know their circumstances or the reasons for their actions. It's also amazing how a few facts can forever alter our perception of a situation. When we feel compelled to judge, it's a good time to ask God for wisdom and patience to understand the facts.

———————————————

Every man should have a fair sized
cemetery in which to bury the faults of
his friends.

HENRY WARD BEECHER

AS TIME GOES BY

> This is the day which the Lord has made; we will rejoice and be glad in it.
>
> PSALM 118:24
> NKJV

"Were does the time go?" we ask. Here it is— a new day on the horizon—and we can't remember how it arrived so quickly. Why, last week seems like yesterday, and last year flew by like a video in fast-forward.

And worse, it's hard to remember what we spent it on.

Shouldn't I have more great memories? we wonder. *What did I accomplish? Is this all I've done with all that time?*

Singer Jim Croce mused in his hit song "Time in a Bottle" that "there never seems to be enough time to do the things you want to do, once you find them." We search so hard for happiness. But often, we don't understand that happiness is not a goal to be won, but a byproduct of a life well spent.

This "Old English Prayer" offers simple instruction for enjoying the day that the Lord has made:

Take time to work, it is the price of success.

Take time to think, it is the source of power.

Take time to play, it is the secret of perpetual youth.

Take time to read, it is the foundation of wisdom.

Take time to be friendly, it is the road to happiness.

Take time to dream, it is hitching your wagon to a star.
Take time to love and be loved, it is the privilege of the gods.
Take time to look around, it is too short a day to be selfish.
Take time to laugh, it is the music of the soul.

True happiness comes from the job
of deeds well done, the zest of
creating things new.

ANTOINE DE SAINT-EXUPERY

A NEW SONG

Singer and songwriter Bobby Michaels tells how one summer he sensed a growing hunger to come up with a new song, but he could not find it within him. As he was visiting his publishing company to discuss a new album, he met a young man working as an intern. The young man mentioned that he wrote songs, and Bobby found himself pouring his heart out to the young man.

"Forget what might be appealing or what might sell," said the young man. "Just tell me what you think God wants you to sing about."

Bobby's story inspired the young man to write a beautiful song that uncannily communicated Bobby's heart. The name of the song is "My Redeemer Is Faithful and True." It is an unpretentious and simple prayer of thanksgiving to our Creator. It is a reverent statement of faith in God's faithfulness. It literally made Bobby's heart sing anew his love for his Savior.

> He put a new song in my mouth, a hymn of praise to our God.
>
> PSALM 40:3

The sales staff and editors did not like the song. In fact, they did not believe that it would sell. "Too slow," they said. "Too redundant." On and on they went. But Bobby remained adamant that this song was directly from God and that it was anointed of God. He was convinced that it ministered to him, and it would minister to others.

Guess what? Bobby was right. God has used the song to bless countless numbers of individuals, and the testimony he gives at his concerts prior to singing the song makes thousands of hearts sing right along with him. And the young man who wrote the song was Steven Curtis Chapman, winner of numerous Dove and Grammy awards.

Isn't God simply amazing! What new song does He want to put in your heart today?

A bird doesn't sing because he has an answer - he sings because he has a song.

JOAN ANGLUND

A REASON TO RISE

While camping deep in the woods, the first sense to attract our attention each morning is . . . smell. The aromatic whiffs of food cooked over an open flame are a wonderful treat to awakening senses. The savory aroma of bacon, sausage, and especially a fresh pot of coffee, gently moves through the forest and rests overhead just long enough to rouse the sleeping camper and produce a memory like no other. Years later campers talk about that experience as if they were reliving it, almost capable of smelling the coffee right then. It's a wake up call campers fondly cherish.

> Arise, shine, for your right has come, and the glory of the Lord has risen upon you.
>
> ISAIAH 60:1 NASB

Each of us has moments like these that provide a platform for memories past that are special to us. These classic times of pleasure linger in our minds, much like the smells of a delicious breakfast on a long ago camping trip. The first call of the morning brings us into the new day and helps to set the pace and tone for the tasks ahead.

Could it be that as followers of Christ, we experience wake-up calls in our lives that are for more than just reminiscing? Our wake-up calls, lessons learned, and "deserts crossed" with God's help and presence, can turn these experiences into opportunities that allow God's loving plans for our lives to shine through us to a lost and depraved world.

Isaiah shouted, "Arise, shine!" Share the joy of knowing Christ with others. There are many who would otherwise never awaken to become a child of God unless you share the joy of knowing Christ with them. Become the aroma of Christ.

A candle loses nothing by lighting
another candle.

PROVERB

YOU ARE ONE OF US

"It's all right; sometimes I don't know why I do things either. You are part of our group, and we support you." With that one statement, the tension evaporated from the room, and other teens expressed their support to Sara.

The setting was a community meeting of adolescents in a mental health treatment facility. Sara suffered from chronic schizophrenia, and she often did not comprehend her actions nor control them. The previous evening, upon returning from a visit home, she had promptly set a small fire in her bathroom that created major problems for the unit, including an evacuation as well as the canceling of evening activities.

> Be ye kind one to another, forgiving one another.
>
> EPHESIANS 4:32 KJV

The next morning, the staff and patients met to work through the problems of Sara's actions and the anger it created among the other teens. For nearly an hour she sat mute in the group as everyone tried to get her to explain. She would not meet anyone's eyes.

But when Sam, another patient, came across the room, knelt down before her, looked up into her face, and expressed his support for her, she responded. Sara told how her mother had become angry with her and screamed at her, "Why don't you just stop being schizophrenic?"

"I just wanted to die; that's why I started the fire," Sara said in a barely audible voice.

Sam's willingness to forgive her in spite of this error in judgment made it safe for Sara to share her heart with the group.

It is the "Sams" of this world who make us a community because of their forgiveness and compassion. For as Saint Francis of Assisi once said, "It is in pardoning that we are pardoned."[16]

Forgiveness is not an occasional act, it is a remanent attitude.

MARTIN LUTHER KING JR.

WHAT'S THE PROBLEM?

Ever had a difficulty that gives you "2:00 A.M. wake-up calls"? It could be a project at work, a committee you've suddenly ended up chairing, or simply the challenge of trying to figure out how to get everything done with only two hands. Whatever the issue, it ruins your sleep and saps your energy for the upcoming day.

The developer of a popular series of business training films describes the phenomenon of discovering your problem-solving skills are going nowhere:

> *You start thinking, I'm uncomfortable. I'm anxious. I can't do this. I should never have started to try. I'm not creative. I was never creative in school. I'm a complete failure. I'm going to be fired, and that means my spouse will leave me and – in other words, you start enjoying a real, good, old- fashioned panic attack.*[17]

Problems can feel ten times as large in the middle of the night. But in reality—and by daylight—solutions might not be as distant as they seem.

> I can do all things through Christ who strengthens me.
>
> PHILIPPIANS 4:13 NKJV

Inventor Charles Kettering had a unique problem-solving method. He would divide each problem into the smallest possible pieces, then research the pieces to determine which ones had already been solved. He often found that what looked like a huge problem was already 98 percent solved by others. Then he tackled what was left.

In bite-sized pieces, problems become more manageable. Remember that, with God, all things are possible. He can give us peace in our darkest nights and bring wisdom with the morning.

Obstacles in the pathway of the weak
become stepping-stones in the pathway
of the strong.

THOMAS CARLYLE

LIKE A NEWBORN BABE

> I will give you a new heart and put a new spirit within you; I will take the heart of stone out of your flesh and give you a heart of flesh.
>
> EZEKIEL 36:26
> NKJV

In 1994, Jim Gleason underwent a life-saving heart transplant at age fifty-one. After he survived one of the most extreme surgeries imaginable, many asked how it felt to live with a new heart. His analogy was "like being born again, but with fifty years of memories and experiences built in."

He tells of coming home just ten days after his transplant. He wanted to go for a short walk around the yard. Accompanied by his daughter, he gazed in wonder at the green grass—so brilliant after weeks of drab hospital room walls. He recalls:

I stopped walking. "Look at that!" I exclaimed to Mary. I was pointing to our small maple tree, so vibrant with the colors of that crisp, clear fall day. Then I spied a grasshopper and, like the young child, exclaimed in glee, "Look at that! A grasshopper!!"

Her response, in disbelief at my reaction, was almost sarcastic, "Well, if that's exciting, look here— a lady bug!"

After four years with his new heart, Jim still cherishes life's simple pleasures. And when is the danger of losing that gift greatest? "As friends and family wish you would return to being 'normal,'" he reflects. "I struggle to never become 'normal' in that sense again."[18]

With God's help, we, too, can walk in newness of life—no surgery required. Give thanks that we don't have to be "normal."

Think not on what you lack as much as on what you have.

GREEK PROVERB

DOUBLE BLESSING

British statesman and financier Cecil Rhodes, whose fortune acquired from diamond mining in Africa endowed the world-famous Rhodes Scholarships, was known as a stickler for correct dress—but not at the expense of someone else's feelings.

> In your godliness, brotherly kindness, and in your brotherly kindness, love.
>
> 2 PETER 1:7 NASB

Once it was told that Rhodes invited a young man to an elegant dinner at his home. The guest had to travel a great distance by train and arrived in town only in time to go directly to Rhodes's home in his travel-stained clothes. Once there, he was distressed to find that dinner was ready to begin and the other guests were gathered in their finest evening clothes. But Rhodes was nowhere to be seen. Moments later, he appeared in a shabby old blue suit. The young man later learned that his host had been dressed in evening clothes but put on the old suit when he heard of his guest's embarrassment.[19]

Rabbi Samuel Holdenson captured the spirit behind Rhodes's gesture, saying:

Kindness is the inability to remain at ease in the presence of another person who is ill at ease, the inability to remain comfortable in the presence of another who is uncomfortable, the inability to have peace of mind when one's neighbor is troubled.

The simplest act of kindness not only affects the receiver in profound ways, but brings blessings to the giver as well. It makes us feel good to make others feel good. So do something nice for yourself today — commit a random act of kindness!

You cannot do a kindness too soon
because you never know how soon it will
be too late.

RALPH WALDO EMERSON

EVERYONE'S A CRITIC

Winston Churchill exemplified integrity and respect in the face of opposition. During his last year in office, he attended an official ceremony. Several rows behind him two gentlemen began whispering, "That's Winston Churchill. They say he is getting senile. They say he should step aside and leave the running of the nation to more dynamic and capable men."

> Let those also who suffer according to the will of God entrust their souls to a faithful creator in doing what is right.
>
> 1 PETER 4:19
> NASB

When the ceremony ended, Churchill turned to the men and said, "Gentlemen, they also say he is deaf!"[20]

Most people find it difficult o ignore the brunt of public opinion. It's easier to do things they don't want to do, or not do what they feel is right, rather than stand up for their own desires and convictions. One writer called it "worshipping the god of other people's opinion."

In the words of Ralph Waldo Emerson:

Whatever you do, you need courage. Whatever course you decide upon, there is always someone to tell you you are wrong. There are always difficulties arising that tempt you to believe that your critics are right. To map out a course of action and follow it to an end requires some of the same courage that a soldier needs. Peace has its victories, but it takes brave people to win them.

Ignoring the god of other people's opinion requires strength and focus. Fortunately, we know the God who can grant us that strength and stand with us as we pursue the paths we feel are right. His opinion is the only one that counts.

Take courage. We walk in the wilderness today and in the promised land tomorrow.

DWIGHT LYMAN MOODY

SENSITIVITY

On the Big Island of Hawaii grows a delicate little plant called Sensitivity, a member of the Mimosa family. Its name is derived from the movement it makes when anything, including a change in the wind, comes near or across it. This minute, spiny-stemmed tropical American plant grows close to the ground. Unless you are directly upon it, you can't distinguish it from grass or weeds in the same area, and it can easily be crushed underfoot.

We all have the built-in need to protect ourselves from danger and those who would harm us. God gave us His Word as a manual to equip us to be aware of the ways of cause it harm. However, Sensitivity can't distinguish between a lawn mower rolling toward it to cut it down or the man coming by to make certain it is protected.

Do not touch my anointed ones.

PSALM 105:15
NASB

As the sun rises in the South Pacific, the tiny Sensitivity plant opens itself as wide as it can and reaches upward toward the warmth of the early morning sunbeams shining down from heaven. This wee drooping plant has a built-in mechanism that causes it to quickly fold itself over and withdraw from anything that might the enemy and to prepare us to know how to protect ourselves.

We can reach up every morning, even when it's

raining or snowing, and receive His warmth, love, protection, and anointing for the day ahead of us. God has blessed us with His sensitivity, but we must be alert and use the tools He has provided for us.

God's way becomes plain when we start walking in it.

ROY L. SMITH

THE MASTER

The story is told of a concert appearance by the brilliant Polish composer and pianist Ignace Jan Paderewski. The event was staged in a great American music hall, where the artist was to perform for the social elite of the city.

Waiting in the audience for the concert to begin were a woman and her young son. After sitting for longer than his patience could stand, the youngster slipped away from his mother. He was fascinated by the beautiful Steinway piano awaiting the performance, and he made his way toward it. Before anyone knew what was happening, he crept onto the stage and climbed up on the piano stool to play a round of "Chopsticks."

The audience was horrified. What would the great Paderewski think? The murmurs quickly erupted into a roar of disapproval as the crowd demanded that the child be removed immediately.

Backstage, Paderewski heard the disruption and, discerning the cause, raced out to join the child at the piano. He reached around him from behind and

The Lord your God in your midst, the mighty one, will save; he will rejoice over you with gladness, he will quiet you in his love, he will rejoice over you with singing.

ZEPHANIAH 3:17 NKJV

improvised his own countermelody to his young guest's "Chopsticks." As the impromptu duet continued, the master whispered in the child's ear, "Keep going. Don't quit, son . . . don't stop . . . don't stop."21

We may never play alongside a master pianist, but every day in our lives can be a duet with the Master. What joy it is to feel His love wrapped around us as He whispers, "Keep going . . . don't stop . . . I am with you!"

We are all strings in the concert of God's joy.

JAKOB BOHME

BRAVEHEART

Kevin tells the story of a dear friend and fellow church member who passed away after a long life of love and service.

> Beloved, thou doest a faithful work in whatsoever thou doest toward them that are brethren and strangers withal.
>
> 3 JOHN 1:5 ASV

At the funeral, his children stood up one by one to tell stories about their father, and soon you noticed a recurring theme: that his single most outstanding trait was his willingness to serve others, no matter what the need. He was one of those people who was always ready to lend a hand — to run an errand, do odd jobs, or give someone a ride home. One of his daughters mentioned how everywhere he went, he kept a toolbox and a pair of coveralls in the trunk of his car, "just in case somebody needed something fixed."

More often than not, when we hear the word courage, we think of heroic acts in times of crisis. But in our everyday lives, we shouldn't overlook the courageousness of simply being there. Lives are changed when we faithfully provide for our families, care for the elderly, or lend an ear to a troubled friend. Persistence in making this world a better place to live — for ourselves and others — is definitely a form of courage.

Albert Schweitzer, the great Christian missionary, doctor, and theologian, was once asked in an interview to name the greatest living person. He immediately replied, "The greatest person in the world is some unknown individual who at this very moment has gone in love to help another."

As you go about your work today, remember that you could be someone else's hero.

———————————

The greatest work any of us can do for
another, whether old or young, is to teach
the soul to draw its water from the wells
of God.

F. B. MEYER

THE VALUE OF DISASTER

For ten years Thomas Edison attempted to invent a storage battery. His efforts greatly strained his finances and, in December 1914, nearly brought him to ruin when a spontaneous combustion broke out in his film room. Within minutes all the packing compounds, celluloid for records and film, and other flammable goods were ablaze. Though fire departments came from eight surrounding towns, the intense heat and low water pressure made attempts to douse the flames futile. Everything was destroyed.

While the damage exceeded $2 million, the concrete buildings, thought to be fireproof, were insured for barely a tenth of that amount. The inventor's twenty- four-year-old son, Charles, searched frantically for his father, afraid that his spirit would be broken. Charles finally found him, calmly watching the fire, his face glowing in the reflection, white hair blowing in the wind.

> We . . . glory in tribulations, knowing that tribulation produces perseverance.
>
> ROMANS 5:3 NKJV

"My heart ached for him," said Charles. "He was sixty-seven—no longer a young man—and everything was going up in flames.

"When he saw me, he shouted, 'Charles, where's your mother?' When I told him I didn't know, he said, 'Find her. Bring her here. She will never see anything like this as long as she lives.'"

The next morning, Edison looked at the ruins and said, "There is great value in disaster. All our mistakes are burned up. Thank God we can start anew." Three weeks after the fire, Edison managed to deliver the first phonograph.22

With each new day, we have the opportunity to start again, to start fresh — no matter what our circumstances. Let the Lord show you how to salvage hope from debris. You never know what joys lie ahead.

Hope is like the sun, which as we journey
towards it, casts a shadow of our burden
behind us.

SAMUEL SMILES

DESTINY:
FIRST CHAIR OR . . .

> In all labor
> there is profit.
>
> PROVERBS 14:23
> KJV

Tony's voice was marked by satisfaction as he spoke of his years in the music industry. "Oh, I could play the trumpet a little bit, and a few other instruments, but as for real talent, I didn't have any. But I do love music and this business."

Over the past thirty years he had been involved with the publication of music and the production of shows in a variety of capacities. But, according to Tony, the most important decision he ever made occurred when he was a trumpet player in a local orchestra.

"I can remember sitting in the orchestra pit looking up at this young guy who handed some papers to the conductor. They talked for quite a while, and the young guy left." The young man was a music arranger, and Tony said, "That changed my life, because I decided right then and there that I wanted to do the same thing."

Over the next several years, Tony pursued and received his undergraduate degree in music with special emphasis on arrangement. He became a successful professional working for a major music publishing company. Today he serves as a manager and leader in the company. As he nears retirement, Tony obviously loves his chosen profession.

William Jennings Bryan once said, "Destiny is not a matter of chance, it is a matter of choice; it is not a thing to be waited for; it is a thing to be achieved."23

Are you at a standstill in your work? Does it feel like a dead end? Are you feeling restless? Ask the Lord to show you a better way to share your talents with the world. He will surely open new doors for you.

Give to the world the best you have, and

the best will come back to you.

UNKNOWN

GUESS WHAT?

"Dad, Dad, guess what, guess what!" she screamed as she bounded into the room and jumped into her father's lap.

"What? What?" he responded with equal vigor and enthusiasm.

One of the greatest joys of his life was seeing his seven-year-old daughter, Crystal's, contagious love of life. In fact, she seemed to attack life with a voracious appetite for discovery unknown to him in any other child.

Before she could respond, he remembered a similar time two years earlier when Crystal came home from school with a brochure that described the coral reefs found in the Florida Keys. At that time she could not read yet, but her teacher had read the brochure to the class, and she remembered it nearly word-for-word. A couple of weeks later, on a glass-bottom boat ride over the reefs, Crystal delighted everyone on board by identifying the types of coral even before the guide could point them out to the group. She wanted to share her newfound knowledge with everyone.

Shaking him from his reverie, Crystal announced with glee, "My picture won first place in the County Art Fair!" His heart was overwhelmed with joy as he shared in her accomplishment. He was so proud of her. But, more importantly, he was so glad that God had blessed his life through her, and he was delighted to hear her news.

God the Father also takes great joy in our accomplishments. Wouldn't it be neat to rush into His presence, jump in His lap, and scream, "Guess what, guess what!" whenever we achieve a life goal? Yes, He already knows, but still, He enjoys our thankfulness and loves our enthusiasm.

―――――――――――――――――――――

Joy is the echo of God's life within us.

JOSEPH COLUMBA MARMION

GRACE TICKETS

A Bible teacher once talked about God's "Grace Tickets." She said God makes himself available to us no matter how many times we reach out for an extra Grace Ticket. His grace is available to us in liberal amounts. She even prayed that she would have the wisdom to know when to reach out and take another.

> The one who comes to me I will certainly not cast out.
>
> JOHN 6:37 NASB

When the alarm goes off at 5:30 A.M., it is all too easy to slip a hand from under the covers and push that snooze button to allow for ten more minutes of sleep. You might repeat the same involuntary movement every ten minutes until 6 A.M., when the clock radio is programmed to come on.

The minute the announcer's voice is heard, you are immediately jolted from bed, realizing you have overslept and must do in twenty minutes what would normally take fifty. The antics that take place in that room are worthy of a feature on a television comedy show.

We all need several of God's Grace Tickets for times in our lives when we attempt to put God and His timing on hold. Yet God has made himself available to us every minute of the day. We are privileged to call out to Him no matter how severe or minuscule our situation. His grace is sufficient for each of us—at all times. He never runs out. It is up to us to open our eyes each morning and reach out to the Giver of all Grace Tickets.

Many of us are in the habit of pushing the "snooze button" on God's time. However, He is patiently waiting with a whole stack of Grace Tickets for us. Why not set your clock by His?

Grace comes into the soul as the morning sun into the world: first a dawning, then a light; and at last the sun in his full and excellent brightness.

THOMAS ADAMS

A PHOTOGRAPHIC MEMORY

Famed photographer and conservationist Ansel Adams was known for his visionary photos of western landscapes, inspired by a boyhood trip to Yosemite National Park. His love of nature's raw perfection is apparent in his stark, mysterious, black and white wilderness photos.

In 1944, he shot a beautiful scene, later entitled "Winter Sunrise: The Sierra Nevada, from Lone Pine, California." It portrays the craggy Sierra mountains in the bright morning sunlight, a small dark horse appearing in the foothills.

But the story is later told that, as Adams developed the negative, he noticed an "LP" carved in the hillside.

Apparently, some local high school teenagers had etched their initials on the mountain.

> If we confess our sins, he is faithful and just to forgive us our sins and to cleanse us from all unrighteousness.
>
> 1 JOHN 1:9 NKJV

Intent on recapturing nature's original, he took a brush and ink and carefully removed the initials from his negative. The man who gave the Sierra Club its look believed in preserving, even perfecting, nature in life as well as in photography.24

Ansel Adams probably never gave a second thought to the unsightly scar on the mountain in his photo creation. In his mind's eye, he saw the beauty of the original and took steps to bring that beauty back into focus.

Someone once observed that "the purpose of the Cross is to repair the irreparable." Through the blood of Christ, we know that our sins have been forgiven—our scars erased—and that once removed, our sins are forgotten. The Lord remembers them no more. When we are willing to confess our sins, He takes joy in restoring us to our original beauty.

The cross is rough, and it is deadly, but it is effective.

A. W. TOZER

SAVED BY THE WEEDS

Farming, like other high-risk occupations, requires a great deal of faith, dependence, and trust in God's timing and goodness.

> Let both grow together until the harvest.
>
> MATTHEW 13:30

One year a potato farmer encountered some problems due to hot weather. Because potatoes are a very temperamental crop and must be in the ground a certain period of time, the farmer was concerned that the planting be done according to schedule.

The weather broke, however, and he planted the potatoes only five days late. As the cultivation program began, everything looked good except for two plots where weeds began to grow out of control two weeks before the harvest. It was too late to destroy the weeds. The farmer had to let them keep growing.

Another more severe problem emerged when a truck strike interfered with the targeted harvest date. The farmer knew that leaving his potatoes too long in the Arizona summer heat would destroy the crop. In the meantime, the "carpet weeds" continued to flourish and provided an almost blanket-like protection over the potatoes, while taller weeds gave additional shade. Later as the harvesters examined the fields, they discovered that wherever the weeds had grown up, there was no spoilage of potatoes. In weed-free areas, the potatoes were ruined because of the heat. The weeds saved his crops. He had only 5 percent spoilage.

God often uses seemingly adverse circumstances to shield and shade us from "spoilage" in our lives. The very "weeds" we chafe about—petty irritations, chronic interruptions, irregular people—are often the means He uses to enhance our ultimate growth and develop a harvest of Godly character in us.

Strength and growth com only through
continuous effort and struggle.

NAPOLEON HILL

CLUBFOOT

Phillip Carey, an orphan and the main character in the novel *Of Human Bondage*, was born with what was once called a "clubfoot." Because of his deformity, his school classmates often made fun of him and excluded him from their boyhood games.

> There was given to me a thorn in my flesh.
>
> 2 CORINTHIANS 12:7 KJV

In one poignant scene, young Phillip is convinced that if he prays hard enough, God will heal his foot. He daydreams for hours about the reaction of his classmates when he returns to school with a new foot: he sees himself outrunning the swiftest boy in his class and takes great pleasure in the shocked amazement of his former tormentors. At last he goes to sleep knowing that when he awakes in the morning, his foot will be whole. But the next day brings no change. He still has a clubfoot.

Although just one of many disappointments for young Phillip, this proves to be a pivotal point in his learning to cope with the harsh realities of his life. Drawing upon an inner strength he did not know he had, he decided that his clubfoot would not determine his destiny. But how he responded to it would make all the difference in his life. If he viewed it as a crippling deformity, he would live a limited life. Instead, he began to see his handicap as nothing more than an obstacle to be overcome, and it did not hold him back.

Life is filled with grand opportunities cleverly camouflaged as devastating disappointments. For Phillip Carey, it was a clubfoot. For the Apostle Paul, it was a thorn in the flesh. Whatever it is in your life, don't despair. With God's help, you, too, can turn your scars into stars, your handicaps into strengths.

Our trials, our sorrows, and our griefs

develop us.

ORISON SWETT MARDEN

THE OLIVE PRESS

In Jerusalem one can stand in the Garden of Gethsemane on the Mount of Olives and look across the Kedron Valley to the Eastern Gate where Scriptures say Jesus will return one day. There in the garden, one of the olive trees is thought to be more than two thousand years old. Perhaps it is the same one Jesus knelt beneath when He agonized in prayer prior to the crucifixion.

> He went away again a second time and prayed, saying, "My Father, if this cannot pass away unless I drink it, thy will be done."
>
> MATTHEW 26:42 NASB

The Israelites were familiar with the procedure of making oil from the olives through a process of pressing that took about three days. Olive oil became a staple used for food and cooking. To this day, virgin olive oil is much favored by gourmet cooks. In biblical times, olive oil was burned in lamps as a source of light. It was used in preservation, anointing, and healing. There is much spiritual significance associated with olive oil. Perhaps it is no wonder that Christ knelt beneath an olive tree as He chose the path of the Cross. When we follow Him, we reflect His love; we are a good seasoning for the world; and we are lights in the darkness. When we place our trust in Him, we are preserved until He comes again.

Today the Garden of Gethsemane is a favorite spot for visitors from around the globe. For each person, regardless of race or religion or background, the olive trees stand as constant reminders of God's grace and redeeming love.

The grace of God is infinite and eternal.
As it had no beginning, so it can have no
end. And being an attribute of God, it is
as boundless as infinitude.

A. W. TOZER

SOUL HUNGER

Despite endless cloudy days this spring, the columbines still managed to bloom. Blue, scarlet, and gold bell-shaped flowers with delicate dangling spurs towered over lacy foliage. They danced gracefully in the breeze, their bright colors attracting hummingbirds. Yet, without God's sun, they didn't seem as radiant as in previous springs.

It is the same with humans. Although we follow our genetic codes and grow into healthy people physically, we have no radiance without the Son of God. The windows of our souls appear cloudy, and God's love cannot shine through us.

Just as columbines hunger for the sun's warm rays, our souls hunger for the loving presence of Jesus. Unlike the columbines, however, we can find the Son even on cloudy days of despair.

We can take action to find the Son by simply reading or listening to His Word and obeying it. We can meet Him in a flower garden, where each stem and blossom appear like signposts to His presence. We can hear His praises being sung by the rustle of leaves held in the tree's uplifted

> The city has no need of the sun nor of the moon to give light to it, for the splendor and radiance (glory) of God illuminate it, and the lamb is its lamp.
>
> REVELATION 21:23
> AMP

branches.

Getting to know Him in a personal way enlightens our souls. His radiance fills our hearts and enlivens our spirits with hope for eternal life with Him in Heaven.

In Heaven, the sun will not be needed because God himself will be our Light. Perhaps Heaven's columbines will always dance with radiance from the glow of God's glory.

The glory of God, and, as our only means
to glorifying him, the salvation of human
souls, is the real business of life.

C. S. LEWIS

LIVING WATER

> If any man is thirsty, let him come to me and drink. He who believes in me, as the scripture said, "From his innermost being shall flow rivers of living water."
>
> JOHN 7:37-38
> NASB

Horticulturists tell us that plants thrive on slow, deep watering that wets the earth to a depth of four to six inches. Then when dry weather hits, the plants are more likely to survive, even if they receive water only once a week. Also, watering in the evening hours decreases the evaporation factor that steals moisture from the plants. One thing is certain, healthy plants that produce lush foliage and beautiful fruit or flowers demand plenty of water carefully applied to their roots. Plant experts say the occasional sprinkling here and there seems to do more damage than good.

Just as plants get thirsty, we get thirsty too. When the Samaritan woman at the well met Jesus, He explained to her that physical water is temporary, but spiritual water is eternal (John 4:13-14). To bear fruit, we need the Living Water of Christ dwelling within. If we're always in a hurry and just read a Bible verse here and there, our roots remain shallow and can wither in dry seasons. Through spending more extended times alone with God in prayer and in reading His Word, we develop inner sustenance for trials that come.

When we let God put His Living Water in our

hearts, not only does He satisfy our spiritual thirst, but He also helps us to grow. And in return, we can be a nourishing fountain to others.

Wherever the son of God does, the winds of God are blowing, the streams of living water are flowing, and the sun of God is smiling.

HELMUT THIELICKE

FROM A TINY SEED

The story goes that a century ago a German princess lay dying. While on her deathbed, she requested that her grave be covered with a large granite slab and that stone blocks be placed all around the slabs to seal the grave. She also gave orders for the granite and stones to be held together with large fasteners made of iron. At her request, the inscription in the top of the stone read, "The burial place, purchased to all eternity, must never be opened."

> Other seeds fell into the good soil and as they grew up and increased, they yielded a crop and produced thirty, sixty, and a hundredfold.
>
> MARK 4:8 NASB

Apparently during the burial, a tiny acorn found its way into the grave. Sometime later, a small shoot began to push its way up through a thin crack in the granite slab. The acorn was able to absorb in just enough nourishment to grow. After years of growth, the mighty oak tree broke through the aging iron clamps. The iron was no match for the oak, and the clamps burst, exposing the grave that was never to be opened. New life sprang forth from a deathbed and one tiny seedling.

Every day we are given numerous opportunities to take advantage of fresh new starts. New beginnings often come when something else has ended. When we allow sin to die in our hearts, we find new life in Christ. Perhaps it is no accident that the mighty oak, which is one of the tallest and strongest trees in the world, starts from a tiny little seed.

What seems to be the end may really be a new beginning.

UNKNOWN

A PATHWAY LIGHT

> Thy word is a lamp to my feet, and a light to my path.
>
> PSALM 119:105 NASB

Most gardens are lighted with small outdoor lanterns that glow just enough to keep visitors from stumbling along the path. At one garden I visited in St. Augustine, Florida, tiny white lights trimmed a centrally located gazebo. Large umbrella-like trees, draped with strings of lights like twinkling diamonds, extended the romantic atmosphere.

Even the smallest light in the right location can illumine a large area. Such is the case in Israel's museum to honor the children who were killed in the Holocaust. Only six candles light the museum. How? Because they are strategically placed in front of various-angled mirrors, magnifying the flames and casting light throughout the rooms.

In the 1800s, a monk named Walter Denham in Belgium placed a candle on top of each one of his well-worn leather shoes. Then with the candles lighted, he could overcome the darkness of the cold stone abbey one step at a time.

Perhaps you are in a set of dark circumstances now—either things you cannot control or habits that you cannot break. You may just feel lonely and empty inside. Just as Walter used the candles to light his physical way, you can find your spiritual way.

Do you need light for your soul today? Relying on God for assistance is like reaching for a lamp in the darkness. As morning light dispels the dark night, the Word of God exposes darkness in our hearts and illumines truth about a Heavenly Father who cares.

Darkness is the absence of light. But since God is Light, then in Him there is no darkness at all.

God is the light in my darkness, the voice
in my silence.

HELEN ADAMS KELLER

FLOWER POWER

Butchart Gardens is one of the most famous tourist attractions in Victoria, British Columbia. The elaborate display dates back to 1904, when Jenny Butchart decided to transform part of her husband's limestone quarry into a sunken garden. Today it is open all year and includes a botanical array of breathtaking beauty.

We dare not make ourselves of the number, or compare ourselves with some that commend themselves: but they measuring themselves by themselves, and comparing themselves among themselves, are not wise.

2 CORINTHIANS 10:12 KJV

When one walks through these delightful grounds, it is impossible to choose the most outstanding exhibition. The plants are obviously healthy and well attended. Each provides colorful blossoms that are distinct, yet make a significant contribution in the overall scheme and design.

Likewise, part of our spiritual growth is to realize our importance in God's garden, especially when we exercise the talents and abilities He has given. Many feel inferior about their own gifts, and they compare themselves unfavorably with others. And yet God designs different people just as He created various kinds of flowers. The lily and the rose each have their own features. In fact, every blossom has its own unique characteristics. Tulips, lilacs, and hyacinths are not alike, yet each kind of flower adds a particular fragrance and beauty to any arrangement.

The same is true in life. Take a few moments to make an inventory of your gifts. Then ask the Holy Spirit to guide you. Through His power, you can make a difference in the lives of others as well as your own.

Give what you have. To someone it may be better than you dare to think.

HENRY WADSWORTH
LONGFELLOW

LIFE LESSONS

You know that what you did was wrong, don't you? The words echoed in Sandra's mind as she went home from school that evening. She was a good student who had never cheated in her life. Yet, this last assignment had been more than she could do. In a moment of desperation, she copied the work of another student.

Her teacher, Mrs. Wallace, had asked her to wait after class, and Sandra knew what was coming. Still, it was a shock when Mrs. Wallace asked her if it was really her work.

Speaking the truth in love.

EPHESIANS 4:15 KJV

"Yes," she squeaked out, then wondered why she had lied.

Looking her straight in the eye, Mrs. Wallace carefully said, "You know that what you did was wrong, don't you? Take tonight to think about your answer, and I will ask you again in the morning if this is your work."

It was a long night for Sandra. She was a junior in high school with a well-deserved reputation for honesty and kindness. She had never cheated before, and now she had compounded her mistake by deliberately lying—and to someone she admired and loved. The next morning she was at Mrs. Wallace's classroom door long before school officially started, and she quietly confessed her misdeed. She received the appropriate consequences, a zero on the assignment and a detention (her first and only detention).

Years later, Sandra often thought of that experience and felt gratitude for loving correction from someone she respected. Mrs. Wallace was willing to help Sandra make honest choices—even on the heels of making a dishonest one. For Sandra, this was a life lesson about taking responsibility for past mistakes and choosing honesty no matter what the consequences.

Sooner or later everyone sits down to a
banquet of consequences.

ROBERT LOUIS STEVENSON

STORYTELLERS

The Polynesians are strong believers in the importance of teaching the next generation the history of their families. They sit around and "talk story." They speak with excitement, and their eyes twinkle as they tell the young ones about their ancestry. The younger generation sits in rapt attention, soaking up every detail. The history of these families is passed down in story form that anyone can easily understand. The children pay special attention so that when they grow up, they will be able to pass the family history down to yet another generation.

A 1998, blockbuster animated film, The Prince of Egypt, tells once again about the Israelites' escape from slavery and their search for a land of freedom and abundance. Modern Jews still tell these same stories as part of their Passover celebration. Traditionally, the youngest child asks why certain foods are eaten and certain traditions are practiced. The answers are told in story form, reflecting on events that occurred thousands of years ago and that have been passed on generation to generation.

Thou shalt teach them diligently unto thy children, and shalt talk of them when thou sittest in thine house, and when thou walkest by the way, and when thou liest down, and when thou risest up.

DEUTERONOMY 6:7 KJV

Jesus taught by telling stories that even the youngest, most uneducated, and least experienced could understand. Now, more than two thousand years later, those parables are still told. Stories about a wayward son, about planting seeds, about searching for a lost coin, and about showing kindness to others are timeless messages about the Kingdom of God.

Aesop's Fables, fairy tales by the Brothers Grimm, and stories by Hans Christian Andersen are memorable, not only for their messages, but also for their interesting characters and events.

If a picture is worth a thousand words, then a story must be worth a thousand pictures. Take time to tell your descendants the amazing story of your life — what God has done in and through you. Impress upon them the importance of sharing this story with future generations so that God's faithfulness will never be forgotten.

History is a story written by the finger of God.

C. S. LEWIS

A GARDEN IN
THE MOUNTAINS

> Why are you anxious about clothing? Observe how the lilies of the field grow; they do not toil nor do they spin, yet I say to you that even Solomon in all his glory did not clothe himself like one of these.
>
> MATTHEW 6:28-29
> NASB

After the mountains of Alaska begin shedding their heavy white coats, the tundra bursts forth in bloom. No one plants flowers on the mountainside, but the bloom of wildflowers is still as predictable as spring itself. Blue lupine, bright pink fireweed, and many other colorful varieties announce that winter has departed. Dark, gloomy days are gradually replaced with more and more light. By midsummer, the days extend almost until dawn. In the twilight's glow, this mountain garden flourishes along endless miles of pristine wilderness.

Every time the sun rises, the seasons change, and the flowers bloom, all of nature seems to be announcing, "God is faithful." In a world of human-made chaos, God is dependable, not only in matters of creation, but in our personal lives as well. Remembering God's dependability is helpful, especially when circumstances are not going our way.

When divorce rips the marriage vows or the doctor diagnoses cancer or the telephone call delivers shocking news, we often wonder if God has forgotten us. Yet when we reflect upon the past events of our lives, we can trace His faithful provision. Just as He adorns the lilies of the field, He will take care of our concerns. So, we need not be anxious. When difficulties arise, we can pray, knowing the Master Gardener is always there, year in and year out.

Just as spring follows winter and renews a harsh landscape, our Jehovah Jireh—the Lord who provides—brings peace to still the turmoil in our hearts and newfound joy with the blessing of each day.

Finding God, you have no need to seek peace, for he himself is your peace.

FRANCES J. ROBERTS

THE BEAUTY
OF DISCIPLINE

The ancient Chinese art of bonsai (pronounced bone-sigh) has existed as a horticultural art form for nearly two thousand years. The word bonsai literally means, in both the Chinese and Japanese languages, "tree-in-a-pot." Practiced all over the world, bonsai is a sublime art where shape, harmony, proportion, and scale are all carefully balanced, and the human hand works in a common cause with nature.

A tree planted in a pot is not a bonsai until it has been pruned, shaped, and trained into the desired shape. Bonsai are kept small by careful control of the plant's growing conditions. Only branches that are important to the bonsai's overall design are allowed to remain, while unwanted growth is pruned away. The bonsai roots are confined to a pot and are periodically clipped.

> Blessed is the man you discipline, O Lord, the man you teach from your law.
>
> PSALM 94:12

The shape of these trees is always as found in nature. Some bonsai have been known to live for hundreds of years, and the appearance of old age is much prized. The living bonsai will change through seasons and years, requiring pruning and training throughout its lifetime. And as time goes on, it will become more and more beautiful.

In truth, the bonsai would be nothing more than

your average tree, but for the discipline of the artist. Giving constant attention to the direction of growth, trimming away what is ugly or unnecessary, and strengthening the most vital branches result in a work of art that brings beauty to its surroundings for many years.

In our own lives, it is that same discipline that makes the difference between an average life and one that brings joy and beauty to its surroundings. With God's Word as our discipline, we, too, can become works of art.

Let God put you on his wheel and whirl you as he likes . . . don't lose heart in the process.

OSWALD CHAMBERS

STRESS AND SERENITY

"Hon," the petite supermarket employee said in her southern drawl, "everybody I know says they are just worn out. " She took a deep breath, brushed a wisp of unruly brunette hair away from her blue eyes, and continued checking groceries.

Stress has become a buzzword for Americans, especially in the last decade. At some point in our lives, we are all overcome with hectic schedules and perfectionistic tendencies.In his article "Confessions of a Workaholic," psychiatrist Paul Meier wrote:

> After he had end the multitudes away, he went up to the mountain by himself to pray; and when it was evening, he was there alone.
>
> MATTHEW 14:23 NASB

Having grown up with an overdose of the Protestant work ethic, I was an honor student who was somewhat overzealous . . . I was a first-class workaholic and I was proud of myself for being one. I thought that was what God wanted of me.[25]

But later through the help of friends, the conviction of theHoly Spirit, and biblical teaching, Dr. Meier established new priorities. At the top of his list was: "Know God personally."

He observed, "I've learned to accept living in an imperfect world. Every need is not a call for my involvement. I have learned to trust God instead of myself to rescue the world. He can do a much better job of it anyway."

Jesus, too, must have been exhausted by demands placed upon Him. When He departed to pray in quiet solitude, He left a significant example for us to follow — daily.

God is a tranquil being and abides in a tranquil eternity. So must your spirit become a tranquil and clear little pool, wherein the serene light of God can be mirrored.

GERHARD TERSTEEGEN

THE GOOD SOIL

> It had been planted in good soil by abundant water so that it would produce branch, bear fruit and become a splendid vine.
>
> EZEKIEL 17:8

An employee approached his employer and said, "I've had ten years of experience on this job, and I'm still making the same salary that I made when I started. It's time that I got a raise."

His boss retorted, "You haven't had ten years of experience. You've had one experience for ten years!"

Many of us feel that our lives could be described in the same way: one experience over and over again—or at best, boringly few experiences. When this is the pattern of our lives, we not only become depressed, but we also have no growth. Just as a garden needs fertilizer and nutrients to enrich its soil, we need the enrichment of activities and experiences to broaden our lives and stimulate our souls.

Joseph Campbell once said, "I don't believe people are looking for the meaning of life as much as they are looking for the experience of being alive."

How, then, may we enrich our lives? It must be intentional. Don't think that someone else can do it for you. There are multitudes of ways to get started:

- Take up a sport that you always wanted to play.

• Take your spouse or a friend out to dinner and the entertainment of your choice.
• Plan a trip to see something or someone interesting.
• Volunteer to do work that will help the less fortunate.
• Visit a friend that you haven't seen for a while.
• Get involved in a place of worship that challenges you.

Participate! Learn! Sing! Read! Praise! Listen! Give! Talk with your God! In experiences such as these, you will find the Source of all the excitement that you can handle.

Experience is the mother of truth; and by experience we learn wisdom.

WILLIAM SHIPPEN JR.

LANDSCAPES

The landscapes around a home are usually very personal and reflect the individual taste of the homeowners. Making the outside reflect the owner is a unique talent landscape architects and novice gardeners have in common. Their work is so admired that friends and neighbors drive by, take pictures, and try to copy what these talented landscape artists create.

Landscaping is indeed an art, but it is also much more. These eye-catching scenes say something about the owner. They express the preferences of the owner, giving insight into what is appreciated and worth all that effort to create.

My beloved brethren, be steadfast, immovable, always abounding in the work of the Lord, knowing that your work is not in vain in the Lord.

1 CORINTHIANS 15:58 NASB

Most gardeners will tell you that even though they love gardening, it's still work. It involves investing money, time, and hard work to create the desired results. For the first year or two, a well-landscaped yard requires just about as much work as a new baby does. But, if you are willing to follow the directions, invest in the necessary materials, feed and water the garden plants, and battle the weeds, you can expect a lovely garden. It takes preparation and commitment—and a lot of hard work.

The way we live our physical lives also expresses who we are and what we appreciate. It takes preparation, the nourishment of the Word, and constant attention to the weeds in our daily lives in order to create a beautiful and satisfying spiritual landscape.

_____

One thorn of experience is worth a whole wilderness of warning.

JAMES RUSSELL LOWELL

FINDING THE
RIGHT "HOME"

A botanist, exiled from his homeland due to political unrest, took a job as a gardener in his new host country in order to support his family. His employer received a unique and rare plant from a friend. There were no care instructions with the plant, so the man put it in one of his hothouses, thinking it would do well there.

> Those who wait for the Lord will gain new strength.
>
> ISAIAH 40:31
> NASB

Only a few days passed when he noticed the plant was dying. He called in his new gardener, the botanist, and asked if he had any ideas that might help to save the plant. The botanist immediately recognized this plant as an arctic variety that needed cold weather in order to survive. He took the plant outside in the frigid winter air and prepared the soil around it so the plant would gradually adjust to its new home. Almost immediately the plant went from wilting to vibrant.

Unaccustomed to the climate in the hothouse, the little plant must have felt the moisture draining from its small veins. The struggle to hold itself up to look the part of an expensive plant gave way under the weary load. The plant began to wilt and became only a shadow of its original beauty.

When the botanist rescued the plant and placed it in an environment suitable to its unique needs, the bowed-down foliage soaked in the nourishment and experienced renewal. Just like that rare plant, we can lose our spiritual strength if we live in an unhealthy environment. Seek God's help to find the right atmosphere for a joyous and productive life.

Spiritual rose bushes are not like natural rose bushes; with these latter the thorns remain but the roses pass, with the former the thorns pass and the roses remain.

SAINT FRANCIS OF SALES

TESTED BY FIRE

Many gardens are outlined by evergreen trees—some large and some small. The lodgepole pine is a tall, stately tree found in the high Western mountains. Commonly seen in Yellowstone National Park, the hard wood of the tree is valuable for making railroad ties and poles. Its fragrant needle-shaped leaves grow in bundles and produce fruit—a woody pine cone—which takes two years to mature.

An interesting feature of the lodgepole is its response to fire. When flames attack the tree, the heat causes the cones to burst. The seeds are then dispersed and natural reforestation occurs. New growth begins, and a fresh forest eventually replaces the charred remains.

During life's trials, the fruit of our lives is also tested. Our spiritual maturity is revealed by how we respond. Do we see God's hand at work, even when our hearts are scorched by pain and sorrow? Have we become intimately acquainted with our Savior so that we know He will somehow use it for good?

> He has said to me, "My grace is sufficient for you, for power is perfected in weakness."
>
> 2 CORINTHIANS 12:9 NASB

When a young child was near death, friends gathered at the hospital to pray with the parents. Another mother, grieving over the loss of her own son, watched the praying group. She later received

Christ as a result of the family's testimony. Both mothers shared a tremendous loss; but they also share a bright hope of one day seeing their boys again in Heaven.

After enduring the fires of adversity, we often learn that others have been watching with powerful results. Through trusting Him, our barren souls burst into life and yield fruit for His glory.

It is not our trust that keeps us, but the God in whom we trust who keeps us.

OSWALD CHAMBERS

THE ROSE AND
THE THORN

There was a very cautious man
Who never laughed or played;
He never risked, he never tried,
He never sang or prayed.
And when he one day passed away
His insurance was denied;
For since he never really lived,
They claimed he never died![26]
UNKNOWN

Progressing through life is so risky, and we all must face it at one time or another. In order to learn to walk, toddlers must risk painful falls time and again. Teens with their first driver's licenses immediately face the most dangerous time of their driving careers. Couples taking the vows of marriage must face the possibility that the very union they expect to bring life's greatest joy could also bring them their greatest heartache. And entrepreneurs trying to launch or expand their businesses know that it could easily bring about a substantial loss.

Samuel grew, and the Lord was with him and let none of his words fall to the ground.

1 SAMUEL 3:19 RSV

Therefore, if there is such potential for pain in our attempts to grow and achieve throughout our lives, why do we even try?

One reason is that God has blessed us with an inner drive that compels us to improve our life. To paraphrase Anais Nin, "The day comes when the risk to remain tight in a bud is more painful than the risk it takes to blossom." And we know that we cannot gather our beautiful roses without the possibility of being pricked by the thorns.

But when the prospect of facing those thorns seems too sharp and painful, remember that as God urges you to reach for new roses, you can also rely on His strength and guidance to help you manage your way through the thorns.

The weaker we feel, the harder we lean on God. And the harder we lean, the stronger we grow.

JONI EARECKSON TADA

"I GOT IT, I GOT IT"

> No discipline seems pleasant at the time . . . however, it produces a harvest of righteousness and peace for those who have been trained by it.
>
> HEBREWS 12:11

"No! No! No! That's not the way," hollered the coach as he watched what seemed like his entire T-ball team chase after the ball and then fight one another for it. While all of the outfielders and half of the infielders joyously wrestled for the baseball, the batter ran from base to base and finally crossed home plate.

The next batter stepped to the plate and promptly lofted the ball toward right center field. Immediately, all four outfielders screamed, "I got it," and the chase for the ball was on again. An instant replay, it seemed.

Again the coach yelled, "Same team, guys, we're all on the same team. Don't fight for the ball!"

Although it did seem like chaos most of the time, the young boys and girls were learning the basics of the game of baseball and teamwork. By the year's end, progress had been made. The fights for the ball with teammates were far fewer, and the players were learning to go to positions to await throws. In fact, at times they even recorded outs.

How did this happen? It happened as the coach applied discipline and enforced rules during practice. At times, the players would get their feelings hurt and even cry when they were not allowed to participate because of misbehavior or unruliness. Yet, they did become better players.

The Christian walk also requires chastening if we are to progress from being unruly children to successful servants. Hannah Whitall Smith says it beautifully: "Look upon your chastening as God's chariots sent to carry your soul into the high places of spiritual achievement."[27]

God, who truly loves, will chastise well.

UNKNOWN

FIRST FRUITS

Gardening opens doors for learning and produces a platform for teaching those around us about God's great provision. Appreciating the elements enough to tackle a garden opens our eyes to God's creativity. Planning helps us to seek and accept God's will for our lives. Tilling the soil and laboring to plant and care for the garden teaches us responsibility and good stewardship. Weeding is a reminder of the spiritual battle we face each day. Waiting for the harvest brings about patience.

Last but not least, reaping the harvest encourages us to be thankful, and sharing the harvest brings blessing to others and honors God.

Throughout history, God's people have been taught to give the first fruits of their harvest as a thanksgiving offering to God. In some cultures, a bountiful harvest is cause for great celebration. In the United States, the Thanksgiving tradition is based on sharing the harvest with others and giving thanks for God's rich blessings.

You shall observe the feast of the harvest of the first fruits of your labors from what you sow in the field.

EXODUS 23:16
NASB

Sometimes the best way to give our first fruits to God means giving to those who are in need from our own abundance. Whether food or money, time or love, we can give what has been given to us. If done cheerfully and generously — with no strings attached — giving the first fruits of our labors brings rich reward.

God showers His blessing upon us, and the cycle of giving thanks and sharing the bounty begins again.

In everything the Lord gives, we can learn principles for our walk with Him if we will allow the lessons to become a part of the gift to us.

The Lord gives his blessing when he finds
the vessel empty.

THOMAS A KEMPIS

GOD'S PLAN

Thomas Edison, probably the greatest inventor in history, once said, "I never did a day's work in my life. It was all fun."

He changed the lives of millions with his inventions of the electric light and the phonograph. He also helped perfect the motion picture, the telephone, and the electric generator. Edison patented more than 1100 inventions in sixty years.

> Then the Lord God took the man and put him into the garden of Eden to cultivate it and keep it.
>
> GENESIS 2:15
> NASB

What was the secret of his success? He defined it himself as "1 percent inspiration and 99 percent perspiration." Perhaps Edison's greatest contribution to modern society was his attitude toward work.

Have you ever thought about the fact that God worked? After He had completed His Creation work in six days, He rested on the seventh. Some people think work was a condemnation upon human beings after Adam's sin. But work was part of Adam's life from the very beginning. God created Adam in His image, and He placed him in the Garden of Eden to cultivate His creation.

Work has its rewards and laziness its consequences. The ant is a good worker. It busily gathers food for the winter without anyone giving a command. In like manner we are to initiate work ourselves and do our best. Paul reminds us not to grow weary of doing good. Work may not always be fun, but it is essential and gives us a sense of accomplishment that nothing else can bring.

Now I wake me up to work,

I pray thee, Lord, I will not shirk,

And if You should come tonight,

I pray You'll find my work's all right.

It is our best work that God wants, not the dregs of our exhaustion. I think he must prefer quality over quantity.

GEORGE MACDONALD

SEASONS

At a dinner party honoring Albert Einstein, a student asked the great scientist, "What do you actually do as a profession?"

Mr. Einstein said, "I devote myself to the study of physics."

The student then exclaimed, "You mean that you're still studying physics? I finished mine last year."[28]

One of the very real temptations of life is to divide it into seasons and then think of each season as an end within itself. Students may think of the high school diploma as the goal and not relate it to what they want to do with their lives. Graduates may get the jobs of their choice and never consider that other jobs could be in their futures.

How often have you seen a young man and woman become engaged to be married, then spend thousands of dollars and hundreds of hours preparing for the wedding, with little or no preparation for the years of marriage ahead? Or, the couple may look forward with great anticipation to the birth of a child, with no plan for proper parenting.

The Garden of Life is a continuing cycle of seasons

and years. Those who reap the greatest harvests seem to look both backward and forward. They look to the past to glean from their experiences those things that will help solve the challenges of today. They look to the future to decide which seeds they should plant today to help them attain their goals for the future.

God is present in every segment of our lives, coaxing us to learn from both our experiences and goals, so that our gardens will reach their full potential.

Though God be everywhere present, yet
he is present to you in the deepest and
most central part of the soul.

WILLIAM LAW

A MIXED BOUQUET
OF BLESSING

Several years ago, Dale Bedford entered the karate tournament as a goal toward receiving his brown belt. But an opponent's kick in the head changed his life direction.

> Every branch that does bear fruit he prunes so that it will be even more fruitful.
>
> JOHN 15:2

At first, his brain trauma was considered only minor, but the blow apparently altered his memory. Like a rose bush completely pruned back to the bare trunk, Dale was forced to start over. His ability level returned to that of a four-year-old. His math and engineering abilities disappeared, as well as his hope for a career in cable-TV engineering.

What did blossom was his artistic talent. The boy who liked to draw some girls and animals in high school and was not considered particularly "good" now supports himself with commissioned oils on canvas, earning up to two thousand dollars per piece. While in therapy at a rehabilitation center, Dale was required to host his own art exhibit of his work.

Dr. Eugene George, professor of neurosurgery at the University of Texas Southwestern Medical Center in Dallas, has treated hundreds of brain-injury patients. He said that it's not uncommon for someone with a brain injury to develop new talents. "There are usually compensations that occur with relearning, and people with brain injuries always tend to re-evaluate what they're doing with their lives," said Dr. George.

For Dale, the accident changed the course of his life. Like a pruned bush, he did more than compensate. With appropriate training and cultivating, and through the touch of the Master Gardener, a pruned bush can produce more beautiful blooms than ever.

Just ask Dale Bedford.[29]

———————————————

All nature, all growth, all peace,
everything that flowers and is beautiful to
the world depends on patience, requires
time, silence, trust.

HERMAN HESSE

FOREVER YOUNG

General Douglas MacArthur once said:

Whatever your years, there is in every being's heart the love of wonder, the undaunted challenge of events, the unfailing childlike appetite for what is next, and the joy and the game of life. You are as young as your faith, as old as your doubt; as young as your self-confidence, as old as your fear; as young as your hope, as old as your despair. In the central place of every heart there is a recording chamber; so long as it receives messages of beauty, cheer, and courage, so long are you young.

We are never too old to learn or to be used for good. We are never too old to be awed by a thing of beauty or to be thirsty for knowledge. Joyful living knows no age limits, and filling our minds with delight in life may in some ways keep us forever young. Our age is not truly measured in physical characteristics and weaknesses, but by our spirit. We are always of value to our Lord. If we are willing to learn new things, develop new skills, and renew our spirits with the nourishment of His Word, we can always grow, regardless of our age.

The growth process never really stops, even when we say we don't want to learn any

> You will be a good servant of Christ Jesus, constantly nourished on the words of the faith and of the sound doctrine.
>
> 1 TIMOTHY 4:6
> NASB

more. Something inside us is always taking in something. Our choice is in whether we allow what we're learning to help us to grow or not.

———————————————————

Be not afraid of growing slowly, be afraid only of standing still.

CHINESE PROVERB

BUSINESS AS USUAL?

Along the Via Dolorosa in Jerusalem are shops with vendors touting their wares. Centuries ago, when Jesus was on His way to Calvary, He trudged along that path, notably called The Way of Suffering.

> He is not here, for he has risen, just as he said.
>
> MATTHEW 28:6
> NASB

Was that day like all others? Was everything business as usual? Farmers bringing in luscious fruit and vegetables larger than you have ever seen; skinned animal meat laid bare, hanging and ready for the butcher. Noise and shouting all around; bargain hunters negotiating the prices. Dark-haired, dark-eyed boys playing loudly in the narrow streets; Roman soldiers scurrying past black-robed Hebrews. "Just another crucifixion," a woman groans while buying a trinket. Were people too busy to even look up when Jesus made that lonely walk along the rugged cobblestones?

Amid the noise and congestion and pressing crowds, one may long for the solitude and peace of the Garden Tomb, where Jesus is believed to have been buried after the crucifixion. Amid the beauty, serenity, overhanging trees, and flowering plants, there rests a holy hush in this sacred place.

You ask me how I know He lives?

He lives within my heart!

From the Via Dolorosa to the Garden Tomb, to living within our hearts, Christ comes to us in victory over death, over sin, over the obstacles of everyday life. Nothing about His life, death, and resurrection is "business as usual." Because He is risen, the world is changed forever.

———————————————

Our Lord has written the promise of the resurrection not in books alone, but in every leaf in springtime.

MARTIN LUTHER

THINKING THINGS THROUGH

One of America's most popular contemporary painters, Andrew Wyeth, portrays life in rural Pennsylvania and Maine so meticulously and naturally that it sometimes appears surreal. A story told by his brother Nat gives a great deal of insight into the source of Wyeth's intensity:

> Andy did a picture of Lafayette's quarters near Chadds Ford, Pennsylvania, with a sycamore tree behind the building. When I first saw the painting, he wasn't finished with it. He showed me a lot of drawings of the trunk and the sycamore's gnarled roots, and I said, "Where's all that in the picture?"

> "It's not in the picture, Nat," he said. "For me to get what I want in the part of the tree that's showing, I've got to know thoroughly how it is anchored in back of the house."[30]

The act of thinking things through is important to every task in our lives. For example, we cannot overlook the importance of good preparation when we are planning our garden, or we risk damaging the plants with poor soil or by setting them too close together to grow freely.

> You care for the land and water it; you enrich it abundantly. The streams of God are filled with water to provide the people with grain, for so you have ordained it.
>
> PSALM 65:9

Wall Street legend Bernard Baruch emphasized this need, stating, "Whatever failures I have known, whatever errors I have committed, whatever follies I have witnessed in private and public life have been the consequence of action without thought."

It is a joy to commune with God and ask His advice as we plan our daily activities. When you have an important task to think through, take time to ask, "Lord, what is Your will?" He will be glad to help.

Four steps to achievement: plan
purposefully, prepare prayerfully, proceed
positively, pursue persistently.

WILLIAM ARTHUR WARD

SHARE THE ABUNDANCE

A farmer whose barns were full of corn used to pray that the poor be supplied, but when anyone in need asked for corn he said he had none to spare. One day after hearing his father pray for the needy, his little son said, "Father, I wish I had your corn."

"What would you do with it?" asked the father.

The child replied, "I would answer your prayer."[31]

Another child must have felt the same way. Supported by the community on Make a Difference Day, twelve-year-old Jessica Burris; her seventeen-year-old brother, Jeffrey; and eleven-year-old friend Corey Woodward collected forty-five hundred pairs of socks and hundreds of other clothes, shoes, blankets, books, and toiletries for people seeking help at free medical clinics.

> A generous man will himself be blessed, for he shares his food with the poor.
>
> PROVERBS 22:9

Others make a difference as well. Twelve men from the United Men of Hollandale in a Mississippi Delta farming area decided to help answer some prayers. In this area, 92 percent of people live in poverty, most jobs and stores are fifteen to twenty miles away, and there is no public transportation. These men serviced eighteen cars for free for single and elderly women who were short on money.

And what about Lynda Duncan? She organized five

hundred volunteers in ten states. Together, they raised $4,246.78 and collected boxes of food, clothes, shoes, and toys for about three hundred needy families. The Duncans gave $1,200 of their own money and delivered four seventeen-foot truckloads of goods to Mountain Outreach, who in turn distributed them to families in the poverty region of Appalachia.[32]

We are blessed, not so that we can tear down our barns and build bigger barns to hold our goods, but so that we can bless others with the abundance of our hearts and lives.

Life is made up, not of great sacrifices or
duties, but of little things, in which smiles
and kindness and small obligations win
and preserve the heart.

HUMPHREY DAVY

RIGHTEOUS FRUIT

The role of quiet places played a very important role in the Bible, especially in the area of faith. Christ was alone during much of His life on earth. He would often retreat from the multitudes for quiet reflection. Moses went alone to the mountain to speak with God. While there, he received the Ten Commandments, one of the cornerstones of our faith. Daniel risked death three times a day, when he would cease from his labors and pray.

> The seed whose fruit is righteousness is sown in peace by those who make peace.
>
> JAMES 3:18 NASB

The Holy Spirit often speaks to us when we are alone. Quiet places produce peace and contentment. Noise breeds confusion. Order is often regained in silence.

Restaurants and other public places have become so congested with noise that it makes some of these places uncomfortable to sit in. Our culture has become so noisy with technology, industry, entertainment, and transportation that we seldom find time and place for quiet. Yet we may yearn for times when we can think, be quiet, and listen to God. Finding time—actually, making time—for the still times is often a daunting challenge.

If righteousness is sown in peace, then the quiet times when we just sit, listen, and wait for the Lord to speak must produce what is essential for spiritual growth. Seeking quiet time for reflection helps us commune with God. As a result, His righteousness wears off on us, and we begin to pick up some of His characteristics.

The Lord has time to spend with us and is ready to grow His Spirit within us. It is up to us to make the appointment.

We all need a secret hideaway where the mind can rest and the soul can heal.

CHERIE RAYBURN

DON'T GIVE UP!

> Let us not get tired of doing what is right, for after a while we will reap a harvest of blessing if we don't get discouraged and give up.
>
> GALATIANS 6:9
> TLB

With the first hint of spring, avid gardeners swoop outside, their arms loaded with seed packets. Then July shatters their enthusiasm with a hammer of one-hundred-degree temperatures. Yet despite the heat, endless clusters of petunias need deadheading, and quack grass slithers across the garden.

August finds the gardeners working long hours in a hot kitchen, canning tomatoes and baking zucchini bread. When the first freeze hits in October, they hustle about the garden digging up the remaining potatoes and mulching the carrots.

By December, the garden is bedded down under a snowy blanket. Warm and snug inside their homes, the gardeners stare out their frosty kitchen windows. Contented sighs whisper through their lips as the pleasure of accomplishment seeps into their souls.

The Christian walk is similar to gardening. In the springtime of our faith, our hearts pound a rapid tempo of plans to save the world.

Summer brings the discovery that our faith requires hard work. We see a need to spend long hours in God's Word to combat inaccuracies in our theology.

When we reach autumn's slower pace in our garden

of faith, we're still working, but we are also beginning to reap the harvest. Come December, we gaze out the window of our souls with a contented, mature love of Christ. Softly exhaling the sigh of a thankful heart, we remember the joy of working with God in His perfectly planned spiritual garden.

Each moment of the year has its own beauty . . . a picture which was never seen before and which shall never be seen again.

RALPH WALDO EMERSON

THE WORRY TREE

There was a man who, at the end of each workday, would visit an old tree in his front yard before entering his home. As he passed the tree, he would reach out to gently touch the trunk and branches.

> Do not worry about tomorrow, for tomorrow will worry about itself. Each day has enough trouble of its own.
>
> MATTHEW 6:34

He did this so he could mentally "hang his troubles" on the branches so that he would not take them inside to his wife and children. He left his troubles with the assumption that if the problems were important, they would still be hanging there when he came out the next morning. But many mornings, he found they had disappeared.

Of course, hanging your troubles on the worry tree is not always easy.

In his book *Still Married, Still Sober*, David Mackenzie describes another practical method for remembering to cast one's cares on God:

> *To act out the principle of turning prayers over to God, we took a paper bag, wrote "God" on it, and taped it up high on the back of our kitchen door. As I prayed about matters such as my career, my role as a father, my abilities to be a good husband, I would write down each concern on a piece of paper. Then those pieces of paper would go in the bag. The rule*

was that if you start worrying about a matter of prayer that you've turned over to God, you have to climb up on a chair and fish it out of the bag. I don't want to admit how much time I spent sifting through those scraps of paper.[33]

Using God as your "Worry Tree" takes practice, but it's a skill worth developing. And your effort will be rewarded with the peace of knowing God is with you, ready to handle your heavy load—if you will only let Him.

Worry is like a rocking chair. It gives you something to do but doesn't get you anywhere.

BERNARD MELTZER

FRIDAY-NIGHT BRAVERY

He was a really skinny, little kid even though he was a junior in high school. And to his younger brother, it was unbelievable how loud Don wheezed when his asthma struck in full force. About once a month, Bobby would be awakened by the sound of Don gasping for breath. Just as soon as he could suck in air, Don would be shaking and gasping for the next breath.

Sometimes their parents would rush him to the emergency room for treatment.

The doctors said that it was the hot, sticky atmosphere or perhaps the smog of the downtown streets that triggered the attacks. They advised Don to stay indoors during the summer months when the humidity was highest. The doctors said that if he stayed indoors, he might be spared from the worst of his attacks.

The problem was that Don and his church youth group had a standing commitment to conduct street revival services every Friday evening, and Don was usually the one to preach. He was determined to never miss an opportunity to fulfill his life calling. So, he continued to preach, no matter the weather, and every once in a while he would fight off the asthma attacks. He counted the cost and decided to take the risk.

> We say with confidence, "The Lord is my helper; I will not be afraid."
>
> HEBREWS 13:6

More than thirty years later, Don is a seasoned missionary in South America. His dedication to sharing the Good News continues to provide inspiration for others. And, he still never misses an opportunity to preach. For his brother, Don's Friday-night bravery still remains a source of encouragement as he, too, grows in his faith.

Trustfulness is based on confidence in God, whose ways I do not understand. If I did, there would be no need for trust.

OSWALD CHAMBERS

NOTHING IS IMPOSSIBLE WITH GOD

Scientists say it can't be done! It's impossible. Aerodynamic theory is crystal clear. Bumblebees cannot fly.

> I can do all things through him who strengthens me.
>
> PHILIPPIANS 4:13 NASB

The reason is because the size, weight, and shape of the bumblebee's body in relation to the total wing spread make it impossible to fly. The bumblebee is simply too heavy, too wide, and too large to fly with wings that small.

However, the bumblebee is ignorant of these scientific facts and goes ahead and flies anyway.

It was God who created the bumblebee and God who taught it how to fly. The bumblebee obviously didn't question God about the problem with aerodynamics. It simply flew. It didn't question whether God really knew what He was talking about. It simply flew. It didn't wonder if God really loved it when He gave it such small wings. It simply flew.

When God created us, He also equipped us for the life ahead. He says He knows the plans He has for our lives. Because He loves us, He has promised to be with us, to teach us, to carry us, and to be our Rock. All we have to do is trust and obey.

God is not limited by our understanding of how things happen. Just because we can't see something, doesn't mean it's not real. Faith is, indeed, the substance of things not seen. Sometimes life is inexplicable, and the impossible happens. We can't always explain everything.

And just because we don't understand how something can be done, doesn't mean our Almighty God can't do it.

God is within all things, but not included;

outside all things, but not excluded; above

all things, but not beyond their reach.

POPE GREGORY THE GREAT

BETTER THINGS
IN MIND

"You just don't want me to have any fun!" Dell shouted as he slammed out of the house and stomped through the backyard. He had no idea where he was going and no way to get rid of his anger, and he was a little nervous that he might be acting childish.

Dell hated the control his parents exercised over him. His friends got to do whatever they wanted, and no one paid close attention to them. They could stay out late and watch whatever movies they wanted, and some of them were dating already. At fourteen, Dell felt he should have the same privileges. What made those other kids so special? Why didn't his parents trust him?

> The Lord disciplines those he loves, as a Father the son he delights in.
>
> PROVERBS 3:12

"Dell?" It was his dad. For a moment, Dell was tempted to ignore him, but he couldn't find the resolve. He turned around reluctantly.

"What?" he asked. He almost missed the football flying through the air and had to quickly throw up his hands to block it. "Geez, Dad!"

He held the pigskin in his hands, tempted to toss it aside. But there was his father, waiting patiently, a smile on his face. Dell swallowed his anger and tossed the ball back. He supposed there could be worse things than having a father who tossed a football around with him, a dad who wanted to keep him pure of heart so that he

QUIET MOMENTS WITH GOD

would do what was right.

How often do you find yourself storming away from God's presence, holding onto something that He has asked you to let go of? How often do you resist His authority because of what your friends are doing? We are not so different from that young teenager, straining for independence. We need to keep in mind that the Father who corrects us knows where we are headed. He wants to keep our vision unclouded, so He can lead us to the life He has set aside for us. Allow God's correction to be the greatest affirmation of His love and hope for your life.

God giveth his wrath by weight, but his
mercy without measure.

SIR THOMAS FULLER

THE HAND OF GOD

Charlie Shedd, author of more than thirty-five books, once told about a time when he felt God's touch. He believes angels have often made themselves known to him by a pressure, a touch, a warning, or an urging. According to Shedd, the Bible often uses "the hand of God" to reveal God's presence.

One evening as Charlie drove into his garage at suppertime, he turned off the automobile ignition but found that his fingers just wouldn't let go. "What's going on here?" he asked out loud.

> He will command his angels concerning you to guard you in all your ways.
>
> PSALM 91:11

An inner voice seemed to say, Go see Roy. From the spot in his heart where he and God conversed, he knew the Holy Spirit was giving a command. Charlie argued, saying, "But it's suppertime." And God's voice seemed to say, Supper can wait, Charlie. Go.

His thoughts ran rampant, but he switched on the ignition and went. But why? he questioned. He'd just seen the senior citizen in church the day before, and he seemed fine. The only response to his question was silence.

Charlie drove to Roy's house less than a mile away, where he found him on the floor, calling for help. He had tripped over a stump, breaking his glasses and cutting his face. Charlie wondered how the elderly man had even made it home; he had injured himself six miles away.

Later, Roy thanked him for coming, then asked, "How did you know I needed you?"

Charlie answered, "I think it was an angel, Roy."

To which Roy promptly responded, "Makes sense. I was lying there on the floor, praying you'd come."

How many times have you heard the quiet voice of the Holy Spirit urging you to respond? How many times have you dismissed Him? Pray this day that God will open your heart to His whisperings and that you will follow His leading to minister to others. If you listen, you will hear Him in the place where you and the Lord hold dialogue.[34]

The voice of God is friendly voice. No
one need fear to listen to it unless he has
already made up his mind to resist it.

A. W. TOZER

UNSPOKEN PRAYER

The kitchen phone jarred Jody's thoughts. "I'll be there as soon as I can," she said, turning off the bubbling stew. Hurriedly, she hung up. "Come on, Tim," she called, "let's go pick up your sister." Her daughter would be waiting outside in thirty-degree weather following the school's choir rehearsal.

Both mother and son shivered as they pulled the car out of the driveway. The heater had finally begun to blow warm air as they rounded a corner and headed up a back street toward the school. Just ahead, under a streetlight, they spotted a small brown-and-white dog, lying motionless. The headlights lit up the dog as Jody slowly drove around the animal. Starting up the hill, she glanced in the rearview mirror.

> Do not be like them, for your Father knows what you need before you ask him.
>
> MATTHEW 6:8

"It moved," she said. "Son, that dog's alive!" She pulled the car over and jumped out, running back. Tears filled her eyes as she allowed the injured animal to smell her hand. "Go get help!" she shouted. "There—at that house!"

Tim raced up to the nearest home and banged on the door. The man who answered, fearful of being bitten by the dog, refused to help and closed the door. When her son explained to her what had happened, she prayed about what to do next. Although her daughter was waiting in front of the school and was probably cold, she was torn by the idea of leaving the dog alone. It was so helpless.

Of the few cars that traveled that back street, none would stop. Then as if God had heard her unspoken prayer, a black sport utility vehicle drove up, and out climbed a man wearing a green medical smock. After checking the injured dog, he said he'd be glad to take it in for treatment. It turned out that he worked for a local veterinarian in town!

On reflection, Jody knew she had felt the real presence of God on that back street late on a cold winter night when the exact person she and the dog needed appeared. How comforting to know the Lord hears our prayers and answers them even before we speak the words! God cares deeply for all His creatures—even injured dogs.

Beware in your prayer, above everything, of limiting God, not only by unbelief, but by fancying that you know what he can do.

ANDREW MURRAY

THE RUSTY NAIL

In the corner of the kitchen, beside the huge oven, an old rusty nail protruded from the wall. It looked as if it had been there for many years. When Cecilia, a gray-haired grandmother, was not in the kitchen, her apron hung securely on that nail. Each time she entered her domain, she immediately reached for her tattered apron and tied it around her waist. It was worn and faded from years of use. Chocolate syrup stains and grease spots covered the huge pockets on the front.

> As the Father has loved me, so have I loved you.
>
> JOHN 15:9

She owned dozens of aprons. Some were made of solid colors, and others were covered with brightly colored designs. Many still had the store tags on them. All of them looked much better than the one that hung on that old rusty nail. When her granddaughter asked her why she preferred the old one to the others, she said that it was a special apron since it was given to her with love. Cecilia never explained why it was so special, but the love it symbolized was evident.

Many years ago, old rusty nails held Jesus Christ on the cross. The need for a sacrifice was what placed Him there. His love for His children is what kept Him there. The King of Kings was reduced to a battered Man as a crown of thorns was placed on His head. And as the rusty nails were driven through His hands, He wept. He focused on His love for us and on His ability to provide the ultimate sacrifice of love. He was worn, much like the old apron. Blood stains covered His body as He said, "It is finished" (John 19:30).

On the third day, the stains were washed away, as Jesus Christ rose bodily from the grave. The scars that were created by the old rusty nails remain visible in the palms of His hands. Those scars represent a kind of love that we can never fully understand, but God's love is obvious as He holds all His children close to His heart.

Where love is concerned, too much is not even enough.

PLERRE-AUGUSTIN DE BEAUMARCHAIS

THE FIRST NEW SHOES

> The king will reply, "I tell you the truth, whatever you did for one of the least of these brothers of mine, you did for me."
>
> MATTHEW 25:40

As the Depression continued, the kitchen cabinets remained empty. Money was scarce. Their father, who had already deserted his family once before, couldn't handle the pressure and left again. As the oldest son, Jerry hit the road to try to earn some money to buy food for his three younger brothers. The air was bitterly cold, and the ground was frozen.

As Jerry walked, he saw some men digging a hole beside the road. "Can I help?" he asked.

"Sure," one of the men said as he handed him a shovel.

Jerry worked hard. For hours he dug in the bitter cold through frozen dirt while sleet pelted the ground. The men handed him a few coins before quitting. The young boy stopped by the corner market to buy some canned goods for Christmas dinner the following day.

As he walked out of the store, the rain and sleet picked up and poured down harder upon him. He had placed cardboard inside his shoes to replace the worn-out soles, and that had worked fine until the freezing water soaked his socks and feet. He sat down on the cold ground to adjust the cardboard.

"Son, are those the only shoes you have?" a man in

uniform asked.

"Yes, sir," Jerry replied.

"Come with me," the man said, and he took him to a shoe store down the street, where he bought him his first pair of brand-new shoes.

The light of Christmas shone brightly at the kitchen table as Jerry's family enjoyed the meal that he had earned the day before, digging a ditch in the freezing cold. The love of Jesus—and the memory of a kind man in a uniform—brought tears to Jerry's eyes as he thanked God for taking care of them all, even in the worst of times.

Love goes without, that another may have.

REV. J. M. GIBBON

THE STORMS OF LIFE

One cold winter day in the 1960s, a major ice storm hit central Georgia. Power outages were rampant throughout the area. Some people owned fireplaces or gas heaters, but others who were less fortunate were forced to seek shelter in the homes of their neighbors.

> We know that in all things God works for the good of those who love him, who have been called according to his purpose.
>
> ROMANS 8:28

One particular family didn't have any source of heat except for the gas stove in their kitchen. For days, while they huddled together around the kitchen table, the heat from the oven kept them warm.

They could cook, while some of their hapless neighbors could not. Many nearby residents brought over cans of soup to heat on their stovetop. Hospitality intensified as a bitter cold spell set in.

Sitting around that table in the glow of a single candle, the family laughed and shared stories and events that were important to each of them. They hadn't done that in months! While the television was out of order, they put their lives back into place. As a result of that storm, the family grew closer. Each one of them remembered the light from that candle for years afterwards.

Sometimes we don't realize what's missing in our lives until we cease all of our busyness. Spending quality family time together is important to God. But you don't need to wait for an ice storm or some other crisis to draw your family close.

God is always faithful to show goodness in every situation. Just as the glow of the candle provided light during the storm, He lights our way through the darkest and most difficult days of our lives.

God is so good that he only awaits our desire to overwhelm us with the gift of himself.

FRANCOIS FENELON

EVENING AND MORNING

In the Book of Genesis, each day of creation is concluded with the phrase, "and there was evening, and there was morning."

> There was evening, and there was morning - the first day.
>
> GENESIS 1:5

From the Hebrew perspective, the day begins at evening, specifically with the setting of the sun. How unlike our Western tradition, where we start our days at the crack of dawn and consider night to be the end of a long day!

What does it mean for the day to begin at evening?

For Hebrew people through the centuries, the transition from afternoon to evening has been marked by prayer. Evening prayer is a Jewish custom. After prayer, families then gather together for a meal.

The most holy day of the week, the Sabbath, begins with the lighting of candles and a proclamation of faith, then a more formal family dinner. After the evening meal, Jewish families traditionally gather together to read God's Word and discuss how His laws apply to their lives. The evening ends in rest.

Consider the priorities evidenced by their way of life:

- They focus upon prayer and their relationship with God.
- They emphasize family life.

- They study the Scripture daily, making God's Word the last thoughts of the day.
- They rest and sleep.

It was only after a Hebrew talked with God, enjoyed the love and fellowship of family, studied the Scriptures, and rested, that work was undertaken!

What would happen in your life if you adopted this strategy for your evening hours? Is it possible you would find yourself more renewed and refreshed, more energetic and healthy, more creative and productive? Might the priorities you desire in your life become a reality?

Why not give it a try? Begin your next day in the evening, and wake up knowing you're totally refreshed—spirit, soul, and body—to have a full and productive day!

———————————

Today is the tomorrow you worried about yesterday, and all is well.

UNKNOWN

NIGHT WATCH

Vaclav Havel is a former president of what used to be Czechoslovakia. In 1948, the Communists took power in his country and confiscated his family land holdings. From that time, Havel was part of a defiant underground that opposed the Soviet government.

> You are my hope, O Lord God.
>
> PSALM 71:5 NKJV

When the Soviets marched into Prague twenty years later, Havel remained to form a coalition that would be ready to take over when the time was right. He spoke out boldly, writing defiantly against communism. He was put under surveillance and eventually jailed for his activities.

In 1970, several United States senators met with Havel in Czechoslovakia. They brought what they thought would be good news for him. They told him they intended to press for legislation allowing dissidents like him to immigrate to the West.

Havel replied by saying he was not interested in going to the West. "What good would that do?" he asked. "Only by staying here and struggling here can we ever hope to change things." Like a watchman in the night, Havel stayed on duty in his country.

Times of trial and struggle often seem like long, dark nights. But doing the right thing—even the hard thing—gives us hope. How do we maintain those long night watches when there seems to be little change in our circumstances?

• Take one step at a time. Don't attempt to tackle the whole task at once. "A man's steps are directed by the Lord" (Proverbs 20:24).
• Keep your struggles in perspective. Separate the mountains from the molehills. "What, then, shall we say in response to this? If God is for us, who can be against us?" (Romans 8:31).
• Cultivate the discipline of delayed gratification. "Let patience have her perfect work, that ye may be perfect and entire, wanting nothing" (James 1:4 KJV).
• Learn to recognize the invisible God in the world around you. "By faith he [Moses] left Egypt, not fearing the king's anger; he persevered because he saw him who is invisible" (Hebrews 11:27).[35]

Placing your hope in the Lord helps you to do all these things. He will lead you; He will remove your mountains; He will strengthen you, helping you to be patient; and He will open your eyes to His works all around you.

If it were not for hope the heart would break.

ENGLISH PROVERB

EARLY TO BED

Most of us are familiar with the old saying: "Early to bed and early to rise makes a man healthy and wealthy and wise." And there are numerous references in the Bible to the joys and benefits of rising early. The psalmist said:

My heart is steadfast, O God, my heart is steadfast; I will sing and give praise. Awake, my glory! Awake, lute and harp! I will awaken the dawn.

PSALMS 57:7-8 NKJV

The clear implication is that the psalmist had a habit of getting up before dawn and "singing in" the morning. But what does this have to do with our sunset hours?

> O God, you are my God; early will I seek you.
>
> PSALM 63:1 NKJV

Very practically speaking, in order to be able to rise early in the morning, we have to get to bed early. There is no substitute for sleep. According to modern sleep research, most people need seven to ten hours of sleep a day, and lost hours can never be made up.

Sufficient sleep is the foremost factor in a person's ability to sustain a high performance level, cope with stress, and feel a sense of satisfaction in life. Getting enough sleep directly impacts our moods and emotions, our ability to think creatively and respond quickly, and our ability to sustain exertion. It is as vital to our health as what we eat and drink.

More good news about sleep and our health is that every hour of sleep we get before midnight is twice as beneficial as the hours after midnight!

A good night's sleep is one of God's blessings to you. Sufficient sleep was a part of His design for your body and His plan for your life. When you make a habit of retiring early, you put yourself in a position to receive this blessing. You'll find it easier to rise early and seek the Lord for His wisdom and strength for the day ahead.

Night is the sabbath of mankind, to rest
the body and the mind.

SAMUEL BUTLER

THE NIGHT SKY

When was the last time you gazed up into the star-filled sky on a clear night? Do you wonder what it would be like to travel in the heavens among the stars? What lies beyond what your physical eyes can see?

> The heavens declare the glory of God; the skies proclaim the work of his hands.
>
> PSALM 19:1

Jamie Buckingham described a night like that in the snowy mountains of North Carolina:

I walked up the dark, snow-covered road toward Cowee Bald. The sky had cleared, revealing a billion stars twinkling in the clear, cold night. The only sound was the gurgling of a small mountain stream beside the road and the soft crunch of my shoes in the snow. All the other night noises were smothered, leaving me with the impression of standing alone on earth.

I wondered about the time, but to glance at my watch would have been sacrilegious. Clocks, calendars, automobiles, and airplanes – instruments of time and speed – were all buried beneath nature's cloak of stillness and slowness. I kicked the snow off my boot, and standing in the middle of the road, threw my head back and breathed deeply of the pine-scented air. Looking into the heavens I could see stars whose light had left there a million years ago and realized I was just glimpsing the edge of space.

Beyond that was infinity — and surrounding it all, the Creator.

I remembered a quote from the German philosopher Kant. Something about two irrefutable evidences of the existence of God: the moral law within and the starry universe above.

I breathed His name: "God."

Then, overwhelmed by His presence, I called Him what I had learned to call Him through experience: "Father!"[36]

Tonight, contemplate the stars in the heavens. You will find there a glimpse of eternity. What an awesome thought: The Creator of the universe invites me to have a personal relationship with Him!

Contemplation is like sleep in the arms of God.

BERNARD OF CLAIRVAUX

EVENING PRAISE

The Book of Common Prayer has a service of Evening Prayer, which includes an ancient hymn called "Phos hilaraon" or "O Gracious Light":

O gracious Light,

pure brightness of the everliving Father in heaven,

O Jesus Christ, holy and blessed!

Now as we come to the setting of the sun,

and our eyes behold the vesper light,

we sing your praises, O God:

Father, Son, and Holy Spirit.

You are worthy at all times to be praised by happy voices,

O Son of God, O Giver of life,

and to be glorified through all the worlds.

> God is light, and in him is no darkness at all.
>
> 1 JOHN 1:5 KJV

This ancient hymn calls our attention to the fact that although the sun may be going down, God's light never leaves us. He is with us always, day and night.

Ancient pagans believed that night was a time of death and sadness, of a "departure of the gods" from the world. This hymn proclaims the exact opposite. Jesus Christ gives life around the clock. The Lather never abandons His children, and He is worthy of praise at all times.

In the book of Revelation, John describes the New Jerusalem, our eternal home, with these words:

There shall be no night there; and they need no candle, neither light of the sun; for the Lord God giveth them light: and they shall reign for ever and ever.

REVELATION 22:5 KJV

Scientists today tell us if anything is reduced to its purest form of energy, it becomes light and heat—the sun in miniature. The Gospel tells us the Son of God is our unending Supply of energy and life.

He is who and what nothing else can provide! He is the Essence of all of life's energy. You can count on Him to bring light, even in your darkest night.

The Lord my pasture shall prepare, and
feed me with a shepherds care; his
presence shall my wants supply, and
guard me with a watchful eye.

JOSEPH ADDISON

FINAL MEDITATION

One of the translations for the word meditate in Hebrew, the language in which the Old Testament was written, is the verb "to mutter" — to voice under one's breath, to continually repeat something. When we are taught to meditate upon the Lord and His Word day and night, we are to repeat God's Word to ourselves continually. When we do this, God's Word becomes foremost in our thinking. It becomes our mindset, our world view, our perspective on life.

The Scriptures promise that when we think and speak in accordance with God's law, we will act accordingly. Thus we will enjoy success and prosperity!

In the opinion of Henry Ward Beecher, a great preacher from the 1800s, "A few moments with God at that calm and tranquil season, are of more value than much fine gold." The psalmist proclaimed, "My mouth shall praise thee with joyful lips: When I remember thee upon my bed, and meditate on thee in the night watches" (Psalms 63:5-6 KJV).

This book of the law shall not depart out of thy mouth; but thou shalt meditate therein day and night, that thou mayest observe to do according to all that is written therein: for then thou shalt make thy way prosperous, and then thou shalt have good success.

JOSHUA 1:8 KJV

Make your last conscious thoughts before sleeping be about God's Word. Turn off the late show, close the novel, put away the work, and rest in the Lord, recalling His Word. You'll find it easier to do this if you choose a passage of Scripture on which to meditate in the morning and then meditate upon it all day — muttering phrases and verses to yourself in the odd moments of your schedule. Then, just before you fall asleep, remind yourself one final time of God's truth.

Those who do this report a more restful night. A peaceful mind focused on God's Word seems to produce peaceful sleep and deep relaxation for the body. In this day and age, with nearly a billion dollars spent each year on sleep aids, we have the greatest sleep aid of all — the Word of God!

Peace: the wisp of straw that binds the
sheaf of blessings.

JEWISH PROVERB

SATISFACTION

"Satisfaction guaranteed!" promise the ads for a new car, a refreshing soft drink, or a stay at an exotic resort. There is no end to the commercial world's promises of fulfilled hopes and dreams.

> In your presence is the fullness of joy.
>
> PSALM 16:11
> NKJV

Do you know many truly satisfied people? Would you describe our culture as satisfied?

If you answer no, you're not alone. Author Max Lucado doesn't think so either. He said, "That is one thing we are not. We are not satisfied."

After Thanksgiving dinner we declare, "I'm satisfied." In reality, we are probably more than satisfied! But before the end of the day's football games, we are back in the kitchen digging into the leftovers.

We plan and save for years for the "perfect vacation." We head off to our dream-come-true destination; indulge every desire for fun, food, and fantasy; and in two weeks we are headed home with wonderful memories. It may have been a satisfying two weeks, but are we fulfilled for the rest of our life when the vacation is over?

Perhaps you worked to build the home of your dreams—the place where you are ruler and reign over every affordable luxury and creature comfort. Does it truly satisfy your deepest desires?

Satisfaction is hard to obtain. Contentment eludes us. We are promised fulfillment many times a day, but the promises become empty after we have "taken the bite" a few times. There is nothing on earth that can satisfy our deepest longing.

In *Mere Christianity*, C. S. Lewis wrote: "If I find in myself a desire which no experience in this world can satisfy, the most probable explanation is that I was made for another world."

We were made for another world—Heaven! The desire for satisfaction is very strong in our lives. However, Scripture tells us there is only one thing that will satisfy: "'For in him we live and move and have our being.' As some of your own poets have said, 'We are his offspring'" (Acts 17:28).

True contentment is the power of getting out of any situation all that there is in it.

G. K. CHESTERTON

HE KEEPS US SINGING

Evangelist and singer N. B. Vandall sat quietly in his living room reading his paper when one of his sons rushed into the house crying, "Paul is hurt! A car hit him and dragged him down the street! He was bleeding all over, and somebody came and took him away."

Vandall found his son at a nearby hospital with serious head injuries, a concussion, and multiple broken bones. The surgeon did not know if he would live. All the distraught father could do was pray as the doctor cleaned and stitched Paul's head wounds and set his broken bones. The rest was up to God.

After coming home to give his family the report, Vandall returned to the living room and fell on his knees with a heartfelt cry of, "Oh, God!" Almost immediately, Vandall could hear God's voice inside him, telling him that no matter what happened in the here and now, all tears will be dried and sorrows will cease in the hereafter. Vandall went to the piano and in minutes wrote a hymn titled "After."

He put a new song in my mouth, a song of praise to our God. Many will see and fear, and put their trust in the Lord.

PSALM 40:3 NRSV

After the toil and the heat of the day,

After my troubles are past,

After the sorrows are taken away,

I shall see Jesus at last.

He will be waiting for me —

Jesus so kind and true;

On His beautiful throne,

He will welcome me home —

After the day is through.

Paul had a near perfect recovery from his injuries, and his father's faith in God remained strong and steady, his gratitude boundless.[37]

God wants to be with you in the midst of your tribulations, too, putting a song of praise in your mouth. When you turn your focus from your struggles to Him, His awesome power can overcome whatever you are facing.

Faith makes the upload good, the outlook bright, the in look favorable, and the future glorious.

V. RAYMOND EDMAN

TIGHTROPE TRUST

In the mid-nineteenth century, tightrope walker Blondin was going to perform his most daring feat yet. He stretched a two-inch steel cable across Niagara Falls. As he did, a large crowd gathered to watch. He asked the onlookers, "How many of you believe that I can carry the weight of a human on my shoulders across this gorge?"

> I know whom I have believed and am persuaded that he is able to keep what I have committed to him until that day.
>
> 2 TIMOTHY 1:12 NKJV

The growing crowd shouted and cheered, believing that he could perform this difficult feat. Blondin picked up a sack of sand that weighed about 180 pounds and carried it across the Falls. They both arrived on the other side safely.

Then Blondin asked, "How many of you believe that I can actually carry a person across the gorge?" Again, the crowd cheered him on.

"Which one of you will climb on my shoulders and let me carry you across the Falls?" Silence fell across the crowd. Everyone wanted to see him carry a person across the gorge, but nobody wanted to put his or her life into Blondin's hands.

Finally, a volunteer came forward willing to participate in this death-defying stunt. Who was this person? It was Blondin's manager, who had known the tightrope walker personally for many years.

As they prepared to cross the Falls, Blondin instructed his manager, "You must not trust your own feelings, but mine. You will feel like turning when we don't need to turn. And if you trust your feelings, we will both fall. You must become part of me." The two made it across to the other side safely.[38]

Jesus gives us the same instruction when we are asked to trust Him in difficult circumstances: "Don't trust your own feelings; trust Me to carry you through."

Courage, brother! Do not stumble, though thy path be dark as night there's a star to guide the humble, trust in God and do the right.

NORMAN MACLEOD

MY KINGDOM FOR SOME SLEEP

> Let us draw near to God with a sincere heart in full assurance of faith, having our hearts sprinkled to cleanse us from guilty conscience.
>
> HEBREWS 10:22

In the recent past, the Internal Revenue Service received an envelope with one hundred $100 bills in it—no name, no address, no note—just money. Someone was feeling guilty.

On another day, the IRS received a large box containing a stack of handmade quilts. The note said, "Please sell these and use the money to settle my tax bill." Since the IRS isn't in the business of selling craft items, the quilts had to be returned.

One man believed he owed the United States District Court $15.43. The court case in question had been held eighteen years earlier, and the man just couldn't wrestle with his conscience any longer. The court insisted that the man didn't owe the money, but he refused to take no for an answer.

Another woman wrote to the IRS and said she felt guilty about cheating on her taxes; enclosed was a check. "If I still can't sleep," she said, "I'll send more." The Bible has much to say about the blessings of a clear conscience and the agony of a guilty one. Perhaps the best example of a man who paid heed to his conscience was David. He made many mistakes, but he always admitted it when he did wrong. He was a man who couldn't sleep until he made peace with his Maker.

"I know my transgressions, and my sin is always before me," he said. "Against you, you only, have I sinned and done what is evil in your sight, so that you are proved right when you speak and justified when you judge" (Psalm 51:3-4).

Are we as honest about our shortcomings as David was?

Confessing our sins brings release from guilt, peace of mind, and sweet sleep. As you retire for the night, check your heart. If you find any unconfessed sin, ask the Lord for forgiveness, and He will give it. He is faithful and just to forgive you from your sins, and He will cleanse you from all unrighteousness. (See 1 John 1:9.)

A man should never be ashamed to own
he has been in he wrong, which is but
saying, in other words, that he is wiser
today than he was yesterday.

ALEXANDER POPE

DEAL WITH IT!

One of the most controversial events in America occurred when Bernard Goetz had had enough and decided he wasn't going to take it any more. He did what many people have wanted to do—he fought back and pulled a gun when he was attacked on the subway.

Goetz's action received an outpouring of support. He touched a nerve in people who have simply had enough of other people threatening their lives. Criticism comes, however, when we allow guns in the hands of angry, violent people. As Christians, anger can be a terrible enemy.

The beginnings of anger almost unnoticed: petty irritations, ordinary frustrations, minor aggravations—things we experience daily. Then these small things start adding up. Pressures build and turn into rage. Without relief, pent-up anger can turn violent, with devastating consequences.

> Be ye angry, and sin not; let not the sun go down upon your wrath.
>
> EPHESIANS 4:26 KJV

How do we keep our passions from becoming uncontrolled anger? How should we defuse the anger that makes us want to retaliate?

There is a righteous, Godly anger that energizes us to take action, to right the wrong, to defend the innocent. However, anger becomes sin when it turns to hate and retribution. Then it is often expressed in inappropriate, destructive ways. We can fly off the handle and act in ways that are as hurtful as what caused us to be angry in the first place. Worse yet, we can store up anger and become bitter and resentful.

There are several things we can do to take control of our anger before it takes control of us:

- Yell at God first! He already knows you're upset.
- Ask God to give you understanding about the situation, to show you the root of your anger, if that's the case.
- Turn the situation over to God. Forgive those who have hurt you, and let Him deal with them. Turn His power loose in the circumstances.
- Don't do anything without having complete inner peace from His Spirit.

Then you can sleep easily at night, knowing God can turn anything around to work for your good.

Control yourself! Anger is only one letter short of danger.

UNKNOWN

CALMING DOWN

It's virtually impossible for you to sleep if you are wound up. Do memories of the day's events keep you from falling asleep? Do you sometimes feel as if you spent the day pushing a boulder up a mountain with a very small stick? If so, memorize these words:

I lift up my eyes to the hills — where does my help come from? My help comes from the Lord, the Maker of heaven and earth.

PSALMS 121:1-2

My sleep had been pleasant to me.

JEREMIAH 31:26

Are you worried about making mistakes, disappointing your boss, or letting your family down? If so, memorize these words:

He will not let your foot slip — he who watches over you will not slumber; indeed, he who watches over Israel will neither slumber nor sleep.

PSALMS 121:3-4

Does unnecessary anxiety sometimes get the best of you, causing you to fear for your own safety or health? If so, memorize these words:

The Lord watches over you — the Lord is your shade at your right hand; the sun will not harm you by day, nor the moon by night.

PSALMS 121:5-6

Are you already starting to agonize over next month's deadline, next year's taxes, the college tuition that has to be paid ten years from now, or funding your own retirement in thirty years? Are you taking all of that on when your head hits the pillow at night? If so, memorize these words:

The Lord will keep you from all harm — he will watch over your life; the Lord will watch over your coming and going both now and forevermore.
PSALMS 121:7-8

You have just memorized an entire psalm! Repeat it to yourself every night. Substitute my for your and me for you. Then rest in the knowledge that God has you, your life, and the rest of the universe under control.

Worry is an indication that we think God cannot look after us.

OSWALD CHAMBERS

UNIQUELY POSITIONED

A number of years ago, IMAX filmmakers produced a movie titled Cosmos. In it, they explored the "edges" of creation—both outer space as viewed through the most powerful telescope, and inner space as viewed through the most powerful microscope. Viewers saw for themselves that at the far reaches of space, clumps of matter (huge stars) seem to be suspended in fixed motion and separated by vast areas of seemingly empty blackness.

They also saw that the same can be said for the depths of inner space—clumps of matter are suspended in fixed orbits, separated by vast areas of seemingly empty blackness. In fact, the world of the distant stars is almost identical in appearance and form to the world of the tiniest neutrinos! Furthermore, neither of these "edges" of creation has been explored fully. Both inner and outer space appear as if they may very well extend into infinity.

In sharp contrast, the created earth as we experience it daily is uniquely suspended between these two opposite poles. Our world is filled with varied colors, dynamic forms, differing patterns, changing seasons,

When I consider your heavens, the work of your fingers, the moon and the stars, which you have set in place, what is man that you are mindful of him?

PSALMS 8:3-4

and adaptable functions.

It is as if God has placed human beings at the very center of His vast creation, with the maximum amount of complexity, meaning, and choice. We are "hung in the balances" literally, as well as figuratively — the pivot point between the great and the small, the vastness of outer space and the vastness of inner space.

We are not only fearfully and wonderfully made, but we are fearfully and wonderfully positioned in God's creation. The Lord has a place for everyone, and specifically, He has a place for you. Thank God for your uniqueness today. Delight in all that makes you special in His eyes. Praise Him for all that He has designed you to be, to become, and to give.

When God conceived the world, that was poetry. He formed it, and that was sculpture. He colored it, and that was a painting. He people it with living beings, and that was the grand, divine, eternal drama.

DAVID BELASCO

WILD PASSION WAVES

Eighteenth-century American poet Fitz-Greene Halleck wrote: "There is an evening twilight of the heart, when its wild passion waves are lulled to rest." How many people long for that moment to come!

For millions of people, the last thoughts of the day are:

> *How can I get people, the last thoughts of the day that thing or person I want? How might I further my own position in this life and capture the success that seems to elude me? How can I overcome my enemy and defeat my adversary?*

According to the Apostle John, such thoughts are "lust of the flesh, and the lust of the eyes, and the pride of life" (1 John 2:16 KJV). Such desires can grow in our minds and hearts until they fill every waking moment. At that level of intensity, they defy sleep, for they require work—our work, our planning, our diligence, our decisions, our effort—in order to bring about a reward that is "our reward," the only kind satisfying to our pride.

> Casting down imaginations, and every high thing that exalteth itself against the knowledge fo God, and bringing into captivity every thought to the obedience of Christ.
>
> 2 CORINTHIANS 10:5 KJV

How might these "wild passion waves" be lulled to rest? John offers this solution: Choose to be impassioned about something else, something eternal. "Love not the world. . . . the world passeth away, and the lust thereof: but he that doeth the will of God abideth for ever" (1 John 2:15,17 KJV). Choose to take captive your thoughts and turn them toward what is eternal and eternally rewarding. If you are going to stay awake in your desire for something, make it a desire for the things of the Lord!

Choose to think about what you might do to further the Lord's Kingdom—for example, a letter you might write to a prisoner, a gift you might give to a person in need, an act of kindness you might render to an elderly friend, or a word of encouragement you might give to a child or teenager. As one preacher said, "Rather than count sheep, count the many ways the Lamb—Jesus Christ—desires for us to love His sheep! The devil will let you go to sleep right away!"

I have a great need for Christ; I have a
great Christ for my need.

CHARLES HADDON SPURGEON

WHAT WOULD YOU SAY?

Standing in line with his squad in the Red Army, Taavi had already made up his mind what he was going to say. The officers made their way toward him, interrogating each soldier down the line with the same question: "Are you a Christian?"

"No," came the answer back.

Then to the next one: "Are you a Christian?"

"No," was the response.

> You are the salt of the Earth . . . you are the light of the world.
>
> MATTHEW 5:13-14 RSV

The young conscripts stood at attention, their eyes fixed ahead. The questioners got closer to the eighteen- year-old Estonian who had been drafted into the Red Army during the Soviet occupation of his country.

Taavi had long been a Christian. Taavi's grandmother had shared her faith with her young grandson. He had accepted the Lord as his Savior, and although he wasn't allowed to attend church, his grandmother taught him what she had learned each week.

The questioners neared. Taavi never really had any doubt what answer he would give. His mind had been made up years before, but he was still nervous. When the officers reached his place in line, they asked, "Are you a Christian?"

Without flinching, Taavi said in a clear voice, "Yes."

"Then come with us," ordered the officers.

Taavi followed them immediately. They got in a vehicle and drove to the building that housed the kitchen and mess hall. Taavi had no idea what was about to transpire, but he obeyed their orders.

The officers said to him, "We are taking you out of combat preparation. You are a Christian, and you will not steal, so we will put you in the kitchen." The kitchen was the biggest black-market operation in the Red Army, with the smuggling and illegal sale of food to hungry soldiers. They knew Taavi's presence would reduce the amount of theft.

When you are challenged for your faith, rise up and boldly proclaim the truth. God will be with you, and He will reward you for your faithfulness.

If we are correct and right in our
christian life at every point, but refuse to
stand for the truth at a particular point
where the battle rages - then we are
traitors to Christ.

MARTIN LUTHER

A DREAM SO FAIR

Thirty men, red-eyed and disheveled, lined up before a judge of the San Francisco police court. It was the regular morning company of "drunks and disorderlies." Some were old and hardened; others hung their heads in shame. The momentary disorder that accompanied the bringing in of the prisoners quieted down, and in that moment of calm, a strange thing happened. A strong, clear voice from below began singing: "Last night I lay a-sleeping; there came a dream so fair."

Last night! It had been a nightmare or a drunken stupor for them all. The song spoke of a contrast that was sharp and convicting: "I stood in old Jerusalem, beside the Temple there."

> (He) showed me the Holy City, Jerusalem, coming down out of heaven from God.
>
> REVELATION 21:10

The song continued. The judge paused. He made a quiet inquiry. A former member of a famous opera company known throughout the nation was awaiting trial for forgery. It was he who was singing in his cell.

Meanwhile the song went on, and every man in the line showed emotion. One or two dropped on their knees; one boy sobbed, "Oh, Mother, Mother!"

The sobs could be heard from every corner of the courtroom. At length one man protested, "Judge," said

212

he, "have we got to submit to this? We're here to take our punishment, but this . . ." He, too, began to sob. It was impossible to proceed with the business of court, yet the judge gave no order to stop the song: "Jerusalem, Jerusalem! Sing for the night is o'er! Hosanna in the highest!"

In an ecstasy of melody the last words rang out, and then there was silence. The judge looked into the faces of the men before him. There was not one who was not touched by the song, not one in whom some better impulse was not stirred.

He did not call the cases singly—he gave a kind word of advice and then dismissed them all. No man was fined or sentenced to the workhouse that morning. The song had done more good than any punishment could possibly have accomplished.

Music has charms to soothe the savage breast, to soften rocks, or bend a knotted oak.

WILLIAM CONGREVE

THE DAY'S ACCOMPLISHMENTS

> In him we live, and move, and have our being.
>
> ACTS 17:28 KJV

If asked whether it's better to be proud or humble, most people would say "humble," since we have been taught that pride is a sin. However, if we think being humble means we are to denigrate ourselves or settle for mediocrity, we have the wrong definition of humility.

Humility is remaining teachable in all situations, knowing God is so much greater and we have so much to learn. Humility comes when we recognize God loves us just the way we are and that He will be patient as we strive to become like Him in character, word, and deed.

Motivational speaker and author Denis Waitley has written:

> *When you come down to the bottom line, joy is accepting yourself as you are right now— an imperfect, changing, growing, and worthwhile person. Realize that liking yourself and feeling that you're an OK individual in your own special way is not necessarily egotistical.*
>
> *Take pride in what you are accomplishing, and even more importantly, enjoy the unique person you are just in being alive right now. Understand the truth that although we as individuals are not born with equal physical and mental attributes, we are born with equal rights to feel the excitement and joy*

in believing we deserve the very best in life.[39]

If you scored a victory today, if you won the prize, if you did the right thing, if you moved beyond yourself and extended an act of love and charity to another human being, rejoice in it! Delight in your awareness that the Lord is working in your life and through your life.

To delight in the Lord's work isn't pride. It's a form of praise to your Father who is proud of you any time you succeed according to His principles and design. All the glory goes to Him. It is because of Him that we can succeed.

The smile of God is victory.

JOHN GREENLEAF WHITTIER

CREATOR GOD

When we see a beautiful piece of art or hear a stirring symphony, we ask, "Who is the artist? Who is the composer?" When we look at the wonders of nature, we are often inspired in the same way, "How did this get here?

W. Phillip Keller writes:

It must be hard for skeptics, atheists, and agnostics to view sunrises and sunsets. The splendor of their glory, the beauty of their colors, the intensity of their inspiration that comes from the Father's loving heart, are to the unbeliever nothing more than mere chemical and physical responses to external stimuli. No wonder their world is so bleak, their despair so deep, their future so forlorn.[40]

The writers of Scripture also saw God in His creation:

The heavens declare the glory of God.
PSALM 19:1 NKJV

The earth shall be full of the knowledge of the Lord as the waters cover the sea.
ISAIAH 11:9 NKJV

God . . . rides through the heavens to your help, and in his majesty through the skies.
DEUTERONOMY 33:26 RSV

Since the creation of the world His invisible attributes are clearly seen.
ROMANS 1:20 NKJV

The morning stars sang together, And all the sons of God shouted for joy.
JOB 38:7 NKJV

Can you see God in the world around you? How big is He to you?

———————————

To him no high, no low, no great, no small; he fills, he bounds, connects, and equals all.

ALEXANDER POPE

AFTER DARKNESS, DAWN

At the turn of the century there was a city worker whose youth had been spent in evil ways. But one night during a revival meeting, he was spiritually born anew. Soon after, he ran into one of his old drinking pals. Knowing his friend needed Jesus, he attempted to witness to him about his newly found peace. His friend rebuffed him rudely and made fun of him for "turning pious."

"I'll tell you what," said the new Christian, "you know that I am the city lamplighter. When I go 'round turning out the lights, I look back, and all the road over which I've been walking is blackness. That's what my past is like." He went on, "I look on in front, and there's a long row of twinkling lights to guide me, and that's what the future is like since I found Jesus."

"Yes," says the friend, "but by-and-by you get to the last lamp and turn it out, and where are you then?"

"Then," said the Christian, "why, when the last lamp goes out it's dawn, and there ain't no need for lamps when the morning comes."

Many children carry their fear of the dark into

> You are a chosen people, a royal priesthood, a holy nation, a people belonging to God, that you may declare the praises of him who called you out of darkness into his wonderful light.
>
> 1 PETER 2:9

adulthood in the form of other kinds of fears—fear of failure, rejection, loss, pain, loneliness, or disappointment. Each of these fears seems to grow in darkness. Darkness is a metaphor for many things: death, night, uncertainty, evil—but in all of them, Jesus is the Light that brings illumination and comfort.

When light shines, not only is darkness eliminated, but fears are relieved as well. Indeed, not only does Jesus give you as much light as you need to proceed in faith, but because of His sacrifice at Calvary, you can be assured of His eternal dawn when the last lamp goes out! Like the lamplighter said, "And there ain't no need for lamps when the morning comes."

O for a closer walk with God, a calm and heavenly frame, a light to shine upon the road that leads me to the lamb!

WILLIAM COWPER

REVIEWING THE DAY

In *You Don't Have to Be Blind to See*, Jim Stovall writes:

> *Your values determine your character, and they set a framework for the choices you make as well as a framework for evaluating your success. In other words, your values provide the framework for self-accountability . . .*

> *Each night before I go to bed, I review the day I've just lived. And I evaluate it. I say about various things I've done or said, and about the choices I've made, "That was good. That was great. That wasn't so hot." In appraising my actions and decisions, I'm able to make midcourse corrections as I pursue my goals. In appraising my deeds of a day, I can close my eyes and have a sense of accomplishment, of being one step closer to the fulfillment of my destiny on earth.[41]*

> This I recall to my mind, therefore have I hope. It is of the Lord's mercies that we are not consumed, because his compassions fail not.
>
> LAMENTATIONS 3:21-22 KJV

Reviewing the day and your values against the criteria of God's Word is a valuable exercise. It allows you to eliminate regret and pride, and you can wipe the slate clean for tomorrow's divine handwriting.

When you recall things about which you have

remorse or sorrow, ask the Lord to forgive you for your sin, give you strength to turn from it, compensate for your errors, and help you to make amends wherever possible.

When you recall things about which you are pleased, give praise to the Lord for the wisdom, strength, and ability He provided throughout the day. Ask Him to use your good deeds and right judgments to expand His kingdom on the earth.

Before bed, put both good and bad in God's hands. You can rest in hope for tomorrow because His mercy and compassion give you a new opportunity to set things right, and you can build on the good, moving forward in His power and love.

Every day should be passed as if it were
to be our last.

PUBLILIUS SYRUS

LETTING GO

The spider monkey is a tiny animal native to South and Central America. Quick as lightning, it is a very difficult animal to capture in the wild. For years, people attempted to shoot spider monkeys with tranquilizer guns or capture them with nets, but they discovered the monkeys were nearly always faster than their fastest draw or quickest trap.

> Forgetting those things which are behind, and reaching forth unto those things which are before, I press toward the mark for the prize of the high calling of God in Christ Jesus.
>
> PHILIPPIANS 3:13-14 KJV

Then somebody discovered the best method for capturing this elusive creature. They found that if you take a clear narrow-mouth glass bottle, put one peanut inside it, and wait, you can catch a spider monkey.

What happens? The spider monkey reaches into the bottle to get the peanut, and it can't get its hand out of the bottle as long as it is clenching the peanut. The bottle is so heavy in proportion to its size, it can't drag it along—and the spider monkey is too persistent to let go of a peanut once it has grasped it. In fact, you can dump a wheelbarrow full of peanuts or bananas right next to it, and it still won't let go of that one peanut.

How many of us are like that—unwilling to change

a habit, be a little flexible, try a new method, or give up something we know is bringing destruction to our lives? We stubbornly cling to our way, even if it brings pain and suffering.

Today, don't cling to a negative situation that may be draining you of your full vitality, energy, creativity, and enthusiasm for living. As the well-known phrase advises, "Let go, and let God!"

Trust the Lord to lead you to the wise counsel and new opportunities He has for you. Have faith in Him to provide what you truly need to live a peaceful, balanced, and fulfilling life. You may never lose your taste for peanuts, but with the Lord's help you can discern when they are trapped in glass bottles!

I asked God for all things so I could enjoy life.

He gave me life so I could enjoy all things.

UNKNOWN

LOOKING BACK

We all know the story of the movie *It's A Wonderful Life*. George Bailey's Uncle Billy loses eight thousand dollars on the day the bank examiner shows up, and George is frantic. In despair, he goes home and looks at his house and family with discouraged eyes. He decides he is a failure at business, his child is sick, his house is all but coming down around his ears — why not just put an end to his life?

> When you are on your beds, search your hearts and be silent.
>
> PSALM 4:4

Thank God for Clarence! Through a series of events, this angel without wings shows George how much his life has meant to his family and friends. Without George, his brother, Harry, would be dead; Mr. Gower; the druggist, would be in prison; his wife would be a frightened old maid; and Bedford Falls would be known as Pottersville — a town as mean and miserable as its namesake.

When George Bailey took an honest look at his life, he could see that despite all the disappointments, there were more than enough triumphs to balance the scales. He had done the best he could, and that had brought tremendous blessing to his family, friends, and community.

Have you had a similar crisis of conscience, a moment when you wondered if your life was worth anything? Take note of these words from Bishop

Thomas Wilson, and ask yourself these questions at the close of each day:

What good am I doing in the world?

Am I bringing up my children to fear God?

Have I been kind and helpful to poor and needy people?

Have I been honest in all my dealings?

Have I lived in the fear of God and worshipped Him both publicly and privately?[42]

The wisest thing to do is keep short accounts. Take stock of your life often. Don't wait for the closing chapter to decide how your book will end!

How endless is that volume which God
hath written of the world! Every creature
is a letter, every day a new page.

JOSEPH HALL

PRINT IT!

When we come to the end of the day and wonder why things went wrong, we usually don't have to look very far to discover the answer. Somehow, we lost our sense of direction and couldn't seem to get back on track. To ensure this doesn't happen again, or at least not as often, we can take some advice from National Geographic photographer Dewitt Jones:

• If there's a problem at work that has you stymied, try looking at it from different points of view. Pray for the eyes of your understanding to be enlightened. (See Ephesians 1:18.) Before he goes out to a shoot, Jones knows he has to have a good camera with the right lens. Different lenses give different perspectives. Jones experiments until he finds the right one.

• Another important factor is focus. A picture can be razor sharp, or if Jones prefers, just the subject in the foreground will be clearly in focus.

• We sometimes become so focused on one aspect of a problem, we lose sight of the big picture— of other circumstances influencing the situation or how the problem is going to affect others if it isn't resolved properly. Look at the big picture, then consider all individuals involved. Jones allows his creative instincts to drive him to find more than one "right" way to shoot a photo. He uses about 400 rolls of film per article—and each published article uses approximately fifty photos.

• Don't be afraid of experimenting with new ideas and methods. Ask God to show you great and mighty things that you haven't known before. (See Jeremiah 33:3.) When Dewitt Jones empties his camera at the end of a shoot, he knows he's given it his best shot. He's looked at the subject he's photographing in as many different ways as he can think of.[43]

If we've found the right perspective; stayed focused on what's truly important; been willing to try something different; and refused to let fear of failure paralyze us; we, too, can look back at our day and say, "Print it!"

No life every grows great until it is
focused, dedicated, disciplined.

HARRY EMERSON FOSDICK

NIGHT LIGHTS

An Illinois pastor had six couples enrolled in a new-members class that met on Sunday evenings in one couple's home. Even after all the couples had completed the course work and joined the church, they continued to meet on Sunday evenings. They enjoyed each other's company and developed a deep sense of commitment to one another.

> You are my lamp, O Lord; the Lord turns my darkness into light.
>
> 2 SAMUEL 22:29

One night, the pastor received a call from one of the wives in the group. Her husband's plane had gone down, and she didn't know if he was dead or alive. The pastor immediately called the other group members, who rallied around her. They sat and prayed with her until word came that her husband was dead. Then various women took turns babysitting and staying with her during those first difficult nights.

Group members opened their homes to out-of-town relatives who came for the funeral. The men kept her car running and did yard work. And when she decided she would have to sell her house and find a smaller place to live, they helped her locate an apartment, pack, unpack, and settle into her new home. For many people, this experience would seem like a night without end, a shadow on their lives that would never be erased. But because her friends let their lights shine into her darkness, they reminded her of the God who understood her pain and promised to see her through it.

"You are the light of the world," Jesus said. "A city on a hill cannot be hidden. Neither do people light a lamp and put it under a bowl. Instead they put it on its stand, and it gives light to everyone in the house" (Matthew 5:14-15).

In a world that seems to grow darker day by day, let the Lord turn your darkness into light. Then you can brighten the lives of those around you by being one of God's "night lights."

I don't have to light all of the world, but
I do have to light my part.

UNKNOWN

HEAVENLY MINDED

"If you read history you will find that the Christians who did most for the present world were just those who thought most of the next," wrote C. S. Lewis.

Recent research bears out this fact. Robert Wuthnow reports, "Christians are more likely to volunteer than other citizens, more prone to give significant time to caring for others, and more likely to believe that they have a duty to do so. Those who attend church regularly, who are active in fellowship and Bible-study groups, who gain a great deal of satisfaction from their religion are far more active volunteers than those who have little church involvement and gain little satisfaction from faith."

One reason why Christians are likely to be involved in helping others is they don't see their life on earth as the sum total of their existence. Instead, they realize that they are actually citizens of another place—Heaven.

> We are his workmanship, created in Christ Jesus for good works, which God prepared beforehand, that we should walk in them.
>
> EPHESIANS 2:10 RSV

They are persons whose Father is in Heaven; their treasure and home are in Heaven. They are born from above, and their affections and attention are set on things above. As citizens of Heaven, they are ambassadors who represent the kingdom of Heaven on earth.

What does it mean to be ambassadors?

- Ambassadors are representatives.

- Ambassadors are foreigners in the country where they are living.

- Ambassadors are only temporary residents of the country where they are living.

- Ambassadors always keep in mind the one they serve; that is their purpose.

- Ambassadors will assist those who wish to immigrate to their country.

Turn your thoughts toward Heaven before sleeping tonight. See how it changes your perspective about your life on earth.

We talk about heaven being so far away. It is within speaking distance to those who belong there.

DWIGHT LYMNAN MOODY

BEYOND THE SUNSET

The ability to see "beyond the sunset" — to anticipate the glories of God's tomorrow — enables a Christian to live joyfully and victoriously in any of life's circumstances.

Virgil P. Brock told how he wrote the beloved hymn "Beyond the Sunset":

> *This song was born during a conversation at the dinner table, one evening in 1936, after watching a very unusual sunset at Winona Lake, Indiana, with a blind guest, my cousin Horace Burr, and his wife, Grace. A large area of the water appeared ablaze with the glory of God, yet there were threatening storm clouds gathering overhead. Our blind guest excitedly remarked that he had never seen a more beautiful sunset.*

> *"People are always amazed when you talk about seeing," I told him.*

> *"I can see," Horace replied. "I see through other people's eyes, and I think I often see more; I see beyond the sunset."*

> *The phrase "beyond the sunset" and the striking*

Now we see but a poor reflection as in a mirror; then we shall see face to face. Now I know in part; then I shall know fully, even as I am fully known.

1 CORINTHIANS 13:12

inflection of his voice struck me so forcibly, I began singing the first few measures. "That's beautiful!" his wife interrupted. "Please go to the piano and sing it."

We went to the piano nearby and completed the first verse. Before the evening meal was finished, all four stanzas had been written, and we sang the entire song together.

The first verse of his beautiful hymn says:

Beyond the sunset, O blissful morning,
when with our Savior heav'n is begun.
Earth's toiling ended, O glorious dawning —
beyond the sunset when day is done.[44]

Live near to God, and all things will appear little to you in comparison with eternal realities.

ROBERT MURRAY MCCHEYNE

FULFILLMENT

Fulfillment is something for which every person seems to long. In its simplest meaning, fulfillment refers to being "fully filled" — having a complete sense of accomplishment.

> I have come that they may have life, and that they may have it more abundantly.
>
> JOHN 10:10
> NKJV

If you lack a sense of fulfillment at day's end, ask yourself, *What did I not do that I felt I should have done?* You'll be calling into question your values, priorities, and goals. As you see areas in which you have fallen short, ask the Lord to help you discipline yourself to achieve what you know is good, adjust your priorities and goals, and refine your values.

A lack of fulfillment isn't the fault of circumstances or another person's behavior. To experience fulfillment, your outer life must be in harmony with your inner life; you must live outwardly what you profess with your mouth and believe in your heart.

For Robert Louis Stevenson, this was the definition of a successful life:

> *That man is a success who has lived well, laughed often and loved much; who has gained the respect of intelligent men and the love of children; who has filled his niche and accomplished his task; who leaves the world better than he found it, whether by an*

234

improved poppy, a perfect poem, or a rescued soul; who never lacked appreciation of earth's beauty or failed to express it; who looked for the best in others and gave the best he had.[45]

Do you have a definition of success against which to gauge your own sense of fulfillment?

There's still time to make today fulfilling. Take a moment to reflect upon your goals, priorities, and values. Ask the Lord to show you where they may need some adjusting. As you rethink these important issues, you will be filled with the knowledge that true fulfillment comes in simply knowing and obeying Him.

———

You have made us for yourself and our hearts are restless until they rest in you.

SAINT AUGUSTINE OF HIPPO

REVERENCE, NOT RITUAL

He said to them, "Why are you troubled, and why do doubts rise in your minds?"

LUKE 24:38

Have you ever met people who, when something good comes their way, start wondering when God is going to take it back?

Long ago, pagans in Germany and Holland believed this way. If Johann met Hans in the forest and said, "Hey Hans! I got that horse I wanted—good price too!" in a second both men would gasp. Johann would run to the nearest tree and start pounding on it.

The pagans believed that the gods lived in trees, and if they heard about any human happiness, they would cause mischief. Johann, realizing his mistake in the listening forest, would rap on trees to drive the gods away. Even when it was no longer a custom to literally "knock on wood," the phrase sufficed to fill the same purpose: "May my good fortune suffer no reversal."

In our lives, it's either "Thy will be done" or "knock on wood." Either God is working for our good, or we must be working for our good.

How sad it must make our Heavenly Father to see us robbed of joy as we receive His blessings, simply out of fear! Furthermore, some people feel the only way to hold onto the joys of life is to perform good deeds. As a result, those parts of the Christian life that should bring us closer to the heart of God often end up as rituals performed out of duty and fear.

When the city of Hamburg was stricken with the plague and large numbers were dying, the healthy—in mortal dread of becoming ill—flocked to the city's churches. It was not a reverence for God that drew them to church, but the fear of cholera. As soon as the plague abated, their zeal for the worship of God also abated.

The Lord desires an intimate, honest relationship with you—not a relationship rooted in your fear of loss or failure. The "fear of God" does not mean you're afraid of God; it means you have respect for Him. This reverence is born out of trust in His love. Turn to Him this evening to experience life, not merely to avoid disaster. When you do, you'll meet a Heavenly Father who loves you completely and unconditionally.

Don't come to the cross out of fear of hell; one to the cross out of love for Christ.

UNKNOWN

A HINT OF ETERNITY

Eternity is a difficult concept for us to grasp. In human terms, it seems a matter of time—or more accurately, timelessness. But eternity is more than a measure of time. Things said to be "eternal" have a quality of permanence. The benefits of eternal things are not found solely in the hereafter; they provide an incredible sense of satisfaction in this life as well.

> We fix our eyes not on what is seen, but on what is unseen. For what is seen is temporary, but what is unseen is eternal.
>
> 2 CORINTHIANS 4:18

The late Lorado Taft, one of America's great artists, often said that a real work of art must have in it "a hint of eternity." The writer of Ecclesiastes says that God has not only made everything beautiful, but also He has set eternity in the hearts of people. (See Ecclesiastes 3:11.) When we do a good piece of work, whether it is part of our vocation or not, we may find in it a hint of eternity, the abiding value that outlasts silver or gold.

Daniel Webster, one of America's most famous statesmen, once said:

If we work on marble, it will perish; if on brass, time will efface it; if we rear temples, they will crumble into dust; but if we work on immortal souls and imbue them with principles, with the just fear of God and love of our fellowmen, we engrave on those tablets something that will brighten to all eternity.

Ascending to the top of one of the magnificent stairways in the Library of Congress, one reads this inscription on the wall: "Too low they build who build beneath the stars."

In building your life, build with God for eternity. In building the Church, build to the glory of Jesus Christ for the salvation of souls.

Ask the Lord to show you this evening how to make your life and effort count for eternity. Pray for an awareness of eternity as you face every decision and task each day.

_____

If we build to please ourselves, we are building on the sand; if we build for the love of God, we are building on the rock.

OSWALD CHAMBERS

FISHING

Once upon a time, fishing was a survival skill. If you wanted to eat, you learned how to fish. Much later it became a form of recreation. In modern times, it has become a sport, with people competing to see who can catch the first fish, the largest fish, the orneriest fish, or the most fish.

For the purist, fishing is still a chance to commune with nature, to become one with the great outdoors. For the first rule of fishing, when you're sitting in a boat in the middle of a lake, is to be quiet! Maybe you can bend this rule in the ocean or while standing in a rushing stream with the water nearly topping your waders, but on a tranquil lake or pond, quiet is imperative.

> Where the river flows everything will live.
>
> EZEKIEL 47:9

For avid fishers, fishing does more than take them away from the noise and confusion of daily life. By just thinking back to previous fishing trips, they can momentarily escape their busy days and stuffy offices.

They can remember the way the sunlight or moonlight looked when it hit the water, the sight of animals or insects going about their business and giving little or no thought to the human in their midst, the satisfaction that came from being alone but not lonely, and the times they chose to share their quiet retreats with one or two friends. Memories such as these are like a park bench in a grove of trees on a cool spring day, a place to lie down and take a deep breath.

In this figurative sense, all of us need a boat in the middle of the lake to escape to now and then. We need a place where we can sit down, throw our lines in the water, and wait patiently for the fish to bite. And if they aren't biting, who cares? As any zealous fisher will tell you, it's not always about filling your bucket. Sometimes, it's about enjoying the warm sun on your head, the wind in your face, and the peace that invades your soul.

Peace is always beautiful.

WALT WHITMAN

FIX YOUR FOCUS

Danish philosopher Soren Kierkegaard addresses the nature of true humility by suggesting we think of an arrow soaring on its course toward its target. Suddenly, the swift-moving arrow halts in mid-flight to see how far it has come, how high it has soared, how its speed compares with another arrow, or to apprehend the grace and ease with which it flies. Right at the moment when it turns to focus on itself, the arrow falls to the ground.

> "I know the plans I have for you," declares the Lord, "Plans to prosper you and not to harm you, plans to give you hope and a future."
>
> JEREMIAH 29:11

Preoccupation with self is counterproductive to reaching our goals. It is the opposite of humility, which is preoccupation with the Lord.

How many times do we compare ourselves to others and measure our success or failure according to someone else's life? The Bible says this is not wise. (See 2 Corinthians 10:12.) The reason God tells us that comparing ourselves to others is not wise is because His plan for our life is totally unique. If we have a question about our life, we should look only to Him.

As for evaluating ourselves, the Bible says we are to examine our hearts, making certain we are walking in faith and purity toward the Lord. (See 1 Corinthians 11:28 and 2 Corinthians 13:5.)

Second Timothy 1:6 exhorts us to stir up the gifts God has given us, and Jesus made it quite clear in the parable of the talents that we are to use all the abilities and resources God gives us to give glory to Him. (See Matthew 25:14-29.)

Whether we are examining our hearts or using the gifts and talents God gave us, our focus is always on the Lord. Our motivation is to please Him, draw closer to Him, and serve those He leads us to serve.

The irony of the Christian life is that when we give our lives to God and to others, we receive true joy and fulfillment. It is when we hold onto our lives and are consumed with our own selfish desires and interests that we are miserable and nonproductive.

Take your mind off yourself, and concentrate on your loving Heavenly Father. Ask Him about His plan for your life.

Trust the past to the mercy of God, the present to his love, and the future to his providence.

SAINT AUGUSTINE OF HIPPO

THE GUIDING LIGHT

> Your word is a lamp to my feet and a light for my path.
>
> PSALM 119:105

Dr. Alexander of Princeton once described a little glowworm that took a step so small it could hardly be measured. But as it moved across the fields at midnight, there was just enough light in its glow to light up the step ahead. As it moved forward, it always moved in the light.

At times we feel lost, like we are stumbling around in the dark. However, the Bible says, "The path of the righteous is like the first gleam of dawn, shining ever brighter till the full light of day" (Proverbs 4:18). Just like the glowworm's path is lit as it continues to take each step, the light of the Word lights our every step.

An Englishman wrote in his diary of an "enlightening" experience he had one dark night: "When I was crossing the Irish Channel one starless night, I stood on the deck by the captain and asked him, 'How do you know Holyhead Harbor on so dark a night as this?'

"He said, 'You see those three lights? All of them must line up together as one, and when we see them so united, we know the exact position of the harbor's mouth.'"

2 Corinthians 13:1 says, "In the mouth of two or three witnesses shall every word be established." The Word of God is one of those witnesses. The perfect peace

of the Holy Spirit is another. And often, God will send a person or a circumstance to confirm we have heard from His Word and His Spirit. When those three "lights" line up, then you know where the "harbor" is.

The Word of God serves as a continuous light to evaluate our daily decisions, much like the light in the Cathedral of Florence. Built by Filippo Brunelleschi, the cathedral stands on marshy ground, so he left a small opening in the dome through which a shaft of light streams every June 21. The sunbeam squarely illuminates a brass plate set in the floor of the sanctuary. Should the ray fail to cover the plate completely, it would indicate the structure had shifted, and steps would need to be taken to deal with the emergency.

The Word of God is the light that tells you if you have shifted off the path God has set for you. Spend some time reading your Bible tonight and every night!

The Bible is meant to be bread for our
daily use, not just cake for special
occasions.

UNKNOWN

THE FATHER'S HEART

"When I was young I admired clever people. Now that I am old, I admire kind people," said Rabbi Abraham Heschel. From the Jewish perspective, an unkind person does not believe in God.

"Flow could anyone who believes in the God of the Bible treat his or her fellow human beings, all of whom are created in God's image, with less than compassion?" asks Rabbi Joseph Telushkin.

"Have we not all one Father? hath not one God created us? why do you deal treacherously every man against his brother?" (Malachi 2:10 KJV).

The story is told that when Abba Tahnah the Pious was entering his city on the Sabbath eve with a bundle slung over his shoulder, he came upon a helpless man lying at a crossroads.

The man said to him, "Master, do an act of kindness for me. Carry me into the city."

Abba Tahnah replied, "If I abandon my bundle, how shall I and my household support ourselves? But if I abandon a man afflicted with boils, I will forfeit my life!"

> I was the eyes to the blind, and feet was I to the lame.
>
> JOB 29:15 KJV

He set down his bundle on the road and carried the afflicted man into the city. Then he returned for his bundle and reentered the city with the last rays of the sun. Everybody was astonished at seeing so pious a man carrying a heavy bundle as the Sabbath was beginning, something forbidden by Jewish law. They exclaimed, "Is this really Abba Tahnah the Pious?"

He too felt uneasy at heart and said to himself: Is *it possible that I have desecrated the Sabbath?* At that point, the Holy One caused the sun to continue to shine, thereby delaying the beginning of the Sabbath.[46]

> *Each kindly act we do toward men,*
>
> *Each loving word by voice or pen,*
>
> *Brings recompense in brotherhood,*
>
> *And makes the Father understood.*[47]

Pray tonight for opportunities to be kind tomorrow. While it may not be on your "to do" list for the day, and may delay a project, your kindnesses toward others count for eternity and show others the nature of your loving Father God.

How beautiful a day can be when kindness touches it.

GEORGE ELLISTON

STRANGERS AND PILGRIMS

> There will be no more death or mourning or crying or pain, for the old order of things has passed away.
>
> REVELATION 21:4

Day in and day out, the details of everyday life can cause our attention to be focused on only the here and now. When change comes—the birth of a child, the first day of school, a new job, the death of a parent—it can be exciting, bittersweet, or even sad.

The first line of a hymn written by Albert E. Brumley gives us the perspective we should have toward the time we spend on this planet. "This world is not my home, I'm just a passing through."

In his book Strangers and Pilgrims, W. R. Matthews describes how we should see ourselves. While he doesn't recommend a total detachment from the life that swirls around us, he advises:

We should live in this world as if we did not wholly belong to it and . . . we should avoid that complete absorption in its vicissitudes into which the most eager spirits easily fall. It is wise to remind ourselves that even our most cherished ambitions and interests are passing; the soul will grow out of them or at least must leave them behind.

To the pilgrim these passages should not be wholly sad. He may feel regret, but not desolation; they do not cause him to rebel. These phases of life are incidents of the journey, but it is the way that matters, not the accidents of the road. The time has come to move on? Then break up the camp with a good heart; it is only one more stage on the journey home![48]

Home, of course, is Heaven, one of the greatest anchors of our Christian life. When we remember our final destination is Heaven, everything we are going through at the moment becomes clearer and more meaningful.

By heaven we understand a state of happiness infinite in degree and endless in duration.

BENJAMIN FRANKLIN

THE POWER OF FORGIVENESS

Unforgiveness is a destructive and insidious force, having more effect on the one who is unforgiving than on the unforgiven. A great example of this was an experience of one of the outstanding intellects of all history, Leonardo da Vinci.

Just before he commenced work on his depiction of the *Last Supper*, he had a violent quarrel with a fellow painter. Leonardo was so enraged and bitter, he determined to use the face of his enemy as the face of Judas, thus taking his revenge by handing the man down to succeeding generations in infamy and scorn.

> If you forgive men when they sin against you, your heavenly Father will also forgive you.
>
> MATTHEW 6:14

The face of Judas was, therefore, one of the first that he finished, and everyone readily recognized it as the face of the painter with whom he had quarreled.

However, when he attempted to paint the face of Jesus Christ, Leonardo could make no progress. Something seemed to be baffling him—holding him back and frustrating his efforts. At length, he came to the conclusion that what was hindering and frustrating him was that he had painted his enemy into the face of Judas.

When he painted over the face of his enemy in the portrait of Judas, he commenced anew on the face of

Jesus. This depiction became a success that has been acclaimed through the ages.

You cannot be painting the features of Jesus Christ into your own life and at the same time be painting another face with the colors of enmity and hatred.

If you are harboring unforgiveness and bitterness, forgive your offender, and put the situation in God's hands. Ask Him to cleanse you of those negative feelings and to release you from their bondage. As you forgive, you will be forgiven and set free to live your life with inner peace.

Forgiveness is man's deepest need and
highest achievement.

HORACE BUSHNELL

PROVIDENCE

February 26, 1844, is one of the most infamous dates in the history of the United States Navy. The most powerful warship of that time, the Princeton, was taking the president of the United States, the secretaries of state and navy, members of Congress, and other government officials down the Potomac.

For the entertainment of the guests, the great gun on the *Princeton*, the Peacemaker, was fired. At the second discharge, the gun burst apart, killing the secretary of the navy and a number of others.

Just before the gun was fired, Senator Thomas Benton of Missouri was standing near it. A friend laid his hand on his shoulder. Benton turned away to speak with him, and much to Benton's annoyance, Secretary of the Navy Gilmore elbowed his way into his place. At precisely that moment the gun was fired, and Gilmore was killed.

That singular moment of providence had a great impression upon Benton. He was a man of anger and feuding and had recently had a fierce quarrel with Daniel Webster. But after his narrow escape from death on the *Princeton*, Benton sought reconciliation with

Webster.

He said to him:

It seemed to me, Mr. Webster, as if that touch on my shoulder was the hand of the Almighty stretched down there drawing me away from what otherwise would have been instantaneous death. That one circumstance has changed the whole current of my thought and life. I feel that I am a different man; and I want in the first place to be at peace with all those with whom I have been so sharply at variance.

Few of us ever know the many times we are spared from death, but in reality each day we live is a gift from God. And no matter how long you live, never waste a day in anger or unforgiveness. Live each day in peace with God and all people.

Forgiveness is a funny thing — It warms the heart and cools the sting.

WILLIAM ARTHUR WARD

FAITHFULNESS

Many people seem to believe God has called them to live successful lives. In reality, He calls each one of us to live faithful lives — lives of obedience, devotion, worship, and service.

With each day there often remains a residue of things left undone, unsaid, unachieved, or unconquered. Each day has its own measure of failure, its own degree of trouble, and its own lingering doubts. (See Matthew 6:34.)

> "The Lord is my portion," says the soul, "Therefore I hope in him!"
>
> LAMENTATIONS 3:24 NKJV

As you conduct a full review of your day — the bad as well as the good — it may be helpful to recall these words by John Oxendale:

"Who Set You There?"

Is your place a small place?
Tend it with care — He set you there.
Is your place a large place?
Guard it with care! — He set you there
Whate'er your place, it is
Not yours alone, but his
Who set you there.

You may not have been as successful today as you

would have liked, but every day you are faithful to the Lord is a success for Him. Remember the things He has promised and that regardless of your performance today, as you give your whole heart to Him, He makes up the difference.

Watch where Jesus went. The one dominant note in his life was to do his Father's will. His is not the way of wisdom or success, but the way of faithfulness.

OSWALD CHAMBERS

PROPER FORM

A father tells a story of an afternoon once spent with his three-year-old daughter. An avid golfer, he was practicing with his clubs in the yard while she played nearby. As he prepared for each swing, he would look to his left to aim the shot, then back to his right to make sure the child was out of harm's way—only then would he take his shot.

> As he who called you is holy, be ye yourselves also holy in all manner of living; because it is written, ye shall be holy; for I am holy.
>
> 1 PETER 1:15-16
> ASV

Soon, he noticed that his daughter was also "playing golf." She had taken a stick to use as a club, and he watched as she set her "club," carefully looked left, then right, then took her shot. In her perception, proper golfing form required that you look both ways before you swing.

Whether we realize it or not, our example leaves an impression on others. In the 1800s, English minister Charles Spurgeon put it this way:

A man's life is always more forcible than his speech. When men take stock of him they reckon his deeds as dollars and his words as pennies. If his life and doctrine disagree the mass of onlookers accept his practice and reject his preaching.

When Jesus said, "You are the light of the world," He wasn't speaking only of our verbal witness. The most profound message we will ever send is the one we live on a day-to-day basis. And it's never more important than when we don't know anyone is paying attention.

Because Someone is always paying attention.

In darkness there is no choice. It is light
that enables us to see the difference
between things and it is Christ who gives
us light.

AUGUSTUS W. HARE

BENEDICTION

A benediction is the pronouncing of a divine blessing. It is usually associated with the final words of a worship service, given by a spiritual leader, but you can give yourself a benediction right where you are, this very night!

The only requirement for a benediction is this: that no sin or unforgiveness stands between you and the Lord Jesus Christ. If you question the purity of your heart, tonight is a good time to ask the Lord to cleanse you and renew a right spirit within you.

> The very God of peace sanctify you and wholly; and I pray God your whole spirit and soul and body by preserved blameless unto the coming of our Lord Jesus Christ.
>
> 1 THESSALONIANS 5:23 KJV

Then face yourself in a mirror before you turn off the lights for the night, and pronounce a benediction upon yourself. Speak it with faith and boldness, in full confidence that the Lord desires this blessing to take root in you and bear good fruit. If you have a family, you may want to pronounce a blessing on them or on each member individually.By doing so, you can end each day with a keen awareness of God's blessing and His claim on your life.

The benediction inscribed at Gloucester Cathedral is one you may want to use:

Go on your way in peace.
Be of good courage.
Hold fast that which is good.
Render to no man evil for evil.
Strengthen the fainthearted.
Support the weak.
Help and cheer the sick.
Honor all men.
Love and serve the Lord.
May the blessing of God be upon you
And remain with you forever.
So be it. And have a blessed good night!

It is distrust of God to be troubled about what is to come; impatience against God to be troubled with what is present; and anger at God to be troubled for what is past.

SIMON PATRICK

FINISHING WELL

Putting the finish on a piece of furniture is the final step in its construction. The bulk of the work that gives the chest, table, or chair its *function* happens much earlier in the process. But it is the finish—the staining and varnishing—that very often gives a piece of furniture its *beauty*. The finish brings out the grain and luster of the wood, the smoothness of the craftsmanship, and the shine that speaks of completion.

> As he had begun, so he would also complete this grace in you.
>
> 2 CORINTHIANS 8:6 NKJV

The cross on which Jesus was crucified marked the end of His earthly life. As He exhaled His last breath, He declared, "It is finished" (John 19:30). This was a triumphant statement that marked the completion of His earthly mission to satisfy and fulfill God's law for all people. The Cross became the beacon that shines brightly into sinful hearts and says, "You can be free." It also became the prelude for a "new beginning" at His resurrection—offering new life for all.

We are each called to end our lives well, but our finish is not simply at our death. It is also in our bringing closure to each day in such a way that we allow for our resurrection the following morning. It is saying with thankfulness and humility, "I've done what the Lord put before me to do today, to the best of my ability. And now, I give my all to Him anew so that He might re-create me and use me again tomorrow."

Ralph Waldo Emerson offered this advice:

Finish every day and be done with it. You have done what you could. Some blunders and absurdities no doubt crept in; forget them as soon as you can. Tomorrow is a new day; begin it well and serenely and with too high a spirit to be cumbered with your old nonsense. This day is all that is good and fair. It is too dear, with its hopes and invitations, to waste a moment on yesterdays.

Amen! The God who began a good work in you will finish it day by day, and ultimately bring it to completion. (See Philippians 1:6.)

Know the value of time; snatch, seize, and enjoy every moment of it. No idleness; no laziness, no procrastination. Never put off till tomorrow what you can do today.

LORD CHESTERFIELD

NO LONGER ENEMIES

The orange kitten was hungry. The grizzly bear was lonely. The man was apprehensive.

The cat weighed no more than 10 ounces when he first slid under the fence into the bear's pen. The man was almost in a panic, thinking the hungry grizzly would kill him with one swat and eat him for dinner.

The grizzly, whose name was Griz, had come to the Oregon wildlife center in 1990, when he was just a cub. Hit by a train while foraging on railroad tracks in Montana, he suffered severe head injuries and was deemed unfit to return to the wild.

The wolf also shall dwell with the lamb, and the leopard shall lie down with the kind; and the calf and the young lion and the fatling together; and a little child shall lend them.

ISAIAH 11:6 KJV

The kitten was one of four kittens abandoned at the center early in the summer. Volunteers were able to find homes for the rest of the litter, but Cat, as he was now called, somehow eluded them.

Then one day in July, Cat turned up in Griz's pen. Afraid to do anything that might alarm Griz, the man just watched, expecting the worst. As the 650-pound grizzly was eating his midday meal, something extraordinary happened. The bear very gently picked out a chicken wing with his forepaw and dropped it near Cat.

From that moment on, Griz and Cat became something of a slapstick animal act. Cat would lay in ambush, then leap out and swat Griz on his nose. Griz would carry Cat in his mouth. Cat would ride on Griz's back, and sometimes Griz would lick Cat.

Their friendly relationship defies both the patterns of nature, as well as their own troubled life histories. Griz never took advantage of Cat's weaknesses, and each animal has accommodated the other's needs.[45]

What a lesson Griz and Cat offer! We can help each other break free from the patterns of our pasts that keep us from loving each other. As we pray for and care for others with the love of Jesus Christ, we obtain healing by the grace of God, both for them and ourselves!

Love is the by-product of our capacity to give what is deepest within ourselves and to receive what is deepest within another person.

LLOYD J. AVERILL

THE EVENING SACRIFICE

The time of the evening sacrifice at the Temple in Jerusalem was from 3:00 to 6:00 P.M. It was during this time period that the unblemished lambs were sacrificed each spring during Passover. The sacrifice was required to be complete before sunset, which was considered the start of a new day.

> Let my prayer be set before you as an incense, the lifting up of my ands as the evening sacrifice.
>
> PSALM 141:2 NKJV

It was also during this time that Jesus gave His life on the Cross outside Jerusalem. The Gospel writers tell us He died after the "ninth hour" (3:00 in the afternoon), and His body was removed from the cross before the official close of the day.

On the cross, Jesus was the unblemished "Lamb slain from the foundation of the world" (Revelation 13:8 NKJV). Christian believers worldwide recognize Him as the perfect Sacrifice for their sins, but Jesus also initiated a "new day" between God and people. Human beings would no longer be separated from God because of sin and guilt, and God could once again have fellowship with those who believed on His Son.

The evening sacrifice marked the end of separation and a new beginning. As you leave your place of work today or move from one set of chores to another, make it a point to say "good-bye" in a tangible way to the day that is past. That may mean closing the office door, turning off the light, or just switching off your pager.

Embrace the new day by leaving the previous day behind. Whatever you have accomplished today is your "sacrifice" of time, energy, ability, and resources to your Lord and Savior. Mark its end with a firm "Amen."

He who runs from God in the morning
will scarcely find him the rest of the day.

JOHN BUNYAN

END-OF-WORK PRAYER

Many people are quick to pray before they eat, before they begin a new project, before they attempt something for the first time, or before they embark on a long journey. They desire to start on the right foot, so they ask for God's help, protection, creativity, and blessing. But oftentimes they forget to pray at the end of a workday, journey, or task.

Such a prayer is like a second bookend on a shelf of freestanding books—it brackets our work and brings us to full recognition that we have received from the Lord the very things we requested. Rather than being a prayer of petition, such a prayer is an expression of praise and thanksgiving.

Simeon had lived his entire life waiting to see the Messiah—a promise the Lord had made to him. (See Luke 2:26.) Upon seeing the infant Jesus in the Temple, Simeon took Him in his arms, blessed God, and said,

> In all your ways acknowledge him.
>
> PROVERBS 3:6
> NKJV

"Lord, now You are letting Your servant depart in peace, According to Your word; For my eyes have seen Your salvation" (Luke 2:29-30 NKJV). Simeon recognized that God had been faithful to His Word, and his heart was encouraged and filled with joy.

Simeon is a wonderful example of how we need to begin and end the events of our lives with prayer. When we reach the end of a day, haggard and weary, we can remember Simeon's prayer, "Lord, let Your servant depart in peace, according to Your Word."

Knowing God was with us today and He will be with us tomorrow, we can move on to the evening hours with freedom and a sense of satisfaction.

Is prayer your steering wheel or your spare tire?

CORRIE TEN BOOM

VANTAGE POINT

Miss Mildred, an eighty-five-year-old resident of Nova Scotia, is a constant reminder to former Undersecretary of the Interior John C. Whitaker that he should not take himself too seriously. She has lived her life in one location, where the population swells to nine in the summer and stays steady at two in the winter.

> Iron sharpeners iron; so a man sharpeners the countenance of his friend.
>
> PROVERBS 27:17 KJV

Whitaker, who has been fishing in Nova Scotia every year since he was twelve, flew in one day for a few hours of recreation. Miss Mildred welcomed him into her kitchen and said, "Johnny, I hate to admit I don't know, but where is Washington?"

When Whitaker realized she wasn't kidding, he explained: "That's where the president of the United States lives—just as the prime minister of Canada lives in Ottawa."

When she asked how many people lived there, Whitaker said there were about two million residents. She responded, "Think of that . . . two million people living so far away from everything."[50]

Our perspective on the world and the actions of others is always seen through our frame of reference, which is shaped by our life experiences. When we must live or work with someone who has a completely different viewpoint, it is easy to be critical.

This is the time when we need to ask God to give us His point of view. Through His eyes, we can see people who are very different from us with more understanding and compassion. The most difficult, frustrating relationships in our lives can be put into a calm and reasonable perspective.

When we ask God to open our eyes to the other person's outlook on life, an interesting thing happens to us. Our own life experiences become richer, and our capacity to relate to others enlarges.

———————————————

O God, help us not to despise or oppose

what we do not understand.

WILLIAM PENN

TO YOUR HEALTH

According to a popular children's song, tea is a "drink with jam and bread." But in a recently released study, nutritionists recommend you have an apple rather than jam and bread with your tea. The Dutch research group found that drinking tea and eating apples together reduces the risk of stroke.

The newly completed study showed health benefits resulted from long-term consumption of black tea — the type most Americans and Europeans drink. Drinking tea, plus eating other fruits and vegetables containing flavonoids, lowered the incidence of strokes. Flavonoids make blood cell platelets less likely to clot and act as antioxidants, which reduce damage to arteries."

> If you have anything against anyone, forgive him.
>
> MARK 11:25
> NKJV

Four-fifths of all strokes result from blood clots, which can lodge in arteries that have been narrowed by damaging oxidation. Flavonoids found in tea and fruit inhibit blood clots and minimize damage to arteries from oxidation, thus allowing a healthy flow of blood and oxygen to the body.

Our spiritual and emotional well being also depend on good circulation: positive thoughts which keep our minds and hearts healthy. Any blockages that would prevent a life-affirming outlook need to be dislodged.

Experts tell us that unforgiveness is one of the biggest obstacles to mental and spiritual health. Author and professor Lewis Smedes outlines four steps to forgiveness:

- Confront your anger; don't deny it.

- Separate the wrongdoer from the wrong. Be angry at the deed, not the doer.

- Let go of the past. Once you have forgiven, you can more easily forget.

- Don't give up on forgiveness—keep working at it. The deeper the hurt, the longer it takes. But keep working at it. You will eventually realize a new attitude.

Smedes adds, "Forgiveness breaks pain's grip on our minds and opens the door to possibility . . . to heal the hurt and create a new beginning."[51]

He that demands mercy, and shows none,
ruins the bridge over which he himself is
to pass.

THOMAS ADAMS

THE STRANGER'S VOICE

> When the morning was now come, Jesus stood on the shore: but the disciples knew not that it was Jesus.
>
> JOHN 21:4 KJV

Some years ago at a resort area along the East Coast, a small community was having an open town meeting about some financial problems they were facing. Among the two dozen or more in attendance was one man no one recognized — a visitor who had apparently dropped in for the meeting. The discussion focused on the desperate state of the town's coffers and on possible ways to raise funds.

During the discussion, the stranger attempted several times to make a comment about various projects being considered, but each time he was interrupted. Eventually, he quit trying and left the hall.

Just as the unknown visitor exited, someone arriving late came into the hall. Out of breath from hurrying, the latecomer asked, "What was he doing here? Is he going to help us?"

The rest asked, "Who are you talking about?"

He said, "You mean you don't know? That was John D. Rockefeller who just left the hall. His yacht is in our harbor. Didn't you get his help?"

In despair someone replied, "No, we didn't get his help. We didn't know who he was."

This true story illustrates two key points:

• Good manners will always have their rewards and rudeness its price.

• We may become so busy trying to find the solution to a problem that we drown out the voice of the Master who has all solutions among His vast resources.

When you are faced with a difficult problem, listen first to what Jesus says to you. No other opinion or solution can ever yield more positive results than His!

A problem is an opportunity to prove
God.

BERTHA MUNRO

HELP OTHERS;
HELP YOURSELF

A tornado rips through a southern town and destroys most of the buildings in its path. Those that remain standing have sustained serious damage, but the owners can't make all of the repairs.

A church in the South has a small congregation and an even smaller budget. Expenses are met each week, but the funds aren't there to hire someone to do minor, but much needed, repairs.

Who comes to the rescue? A group of mostly retirees in recreational vehicles. They travel throughout the South during the autumn and winter months, escaping cold temperatures and doing good along the way. Some are experienced in carpentry and construction, and some are not, but they all have the same goal: to make their time count by helping others.

> As the body without the spirit is dead, so faith without works is dead also.
>
> JAMES 2:26 KJV

The United Methodist Church chooses projects and assigns teams to each site. The workers, who pay all their expenses, meet at the appointed time and get right to work. To keep the jobs enjoyable, everyone works four days and then has three days off to relax and see the sights. The fun part, reported one woman volunteer, is the opportunity to have fellowship with like-minded people.[52]

The same generosity of spirit, on a slightly different scale, is described in the Book of Acts. "All the believers were one in heart and mind. No one claimed that any of his possessions was his own, but they shared everything they had. There were no needy persons among them. For from time to time those who owned lands or houses sold them, brought the money from the sales and put it at the apostles' feet, and it was distributed to anyone as he had need" (Acts 4:32, 34-35).

When we have the chance to do good, we should jump at it. "In everything, do to others what you would have them do to you, for this sums up the Law and the Prophets," Jesus said in Matthew 7:12. Jesus asked us to serve, and we will be blessed when we do so.

No act of kindness, no matter how small,
is ever wasted.

AESOP

THE MIRACLE OF
A KIND WORD

Rev. Purnell Bailey tells of a convict from Darlington, England, who had just been released from prison. He had spent three long years in prison for embezzlement, and though he wanted to return to his hometown, he was concerned about the social ostracism and possible ridicule he might have to endure from some of the townsfolk. Still, he was lonesome for his home and decided to risk the worst.

> Thou has lifted me up, and hast not made my foes to rejoice over me.
>
> PSALM 30:1 KJV

He had barely set foot on the main street of town when he encountered the mayor himself.

"Hello!" greeted the mayor in a cheery voice. "I'm glad to see you! How are you?" The man appeared ill at ease, and so the mayor moved on.

Years later, the former mayor and the ex-convict accidentally met in another town. The latter said, "I want you to know what you did for me when I came out of prison."

"What did I do?" asked the mayor.

"You spoke a kind word to me and changed my life," replied the grateful man.[53]

We cannot always know how important the seed of a kind word may be to the one who receives it. More often than we know, words of encouragement or recognition provide a turning point in a person's outlook on life.

Just as Jesus spoke with love and acceptance to the hated tax collector Zaccheus, the mayor set the tone for others' contacts with the ex-convict by openly and warmly addressing him as a neighbor. People watch those they respect for cues regarding their own relationships with certain people.

Genuine, kind words cost the giver nothing, but they can mean the world to the one receiving them. Today, don't be put off when someone to whom you offer a kind word seems uncomfortable or embarrassed. Recognize they may be unpracticed at receiving love and compassion, even though they need it greatly.

Kind words toward those you daily meet,
kind words and actions right, will make
this life of ours most sweet, turn
darkness into light.

ISAAC WATTS

OUR EVERYTHING

World-famous orchestra conductor Arturo Toscanini was very exacting and almost tyrannical in rehearsals, but the musicians who played with him and his audiences never doubted his focus.

> Christ is all, and is in all.
>
> COLOSSIANS 3:11

To prepare for a performance of *Beethoven's Ninth Symphony*, he rehearsed each section of instruments separately. They played their parts over and over again until he was satisfied. Finally the sections were joined together.

The date arrived for the performance of this master symphony. The orchestra performed superbly, inspired by Toscanini's demanding artistic leadership. At the close of the concert, the first violinist said to the musician next to him, "If he scolds us after that, I will jump up and push him off the platform."

Toscanini did not scold the musicians nor critique their performance in any way. Instead he stood silent with arms outstretched, his deep-set eyes burning with an inner fire, the light of a great rapture upon his face, and a spirit of utter contentment enfolding him. After along silence, he said, "Who am I? Who is Toscanini? Who are you? I am nobody! You are nobody!"

The crowded concert hall was hushed. The master conductor remained with his arms extended, and the audience and orchestra waited in awe. Then, his face beaming with the light of one who has seen a vision, he added, "Beethoven is everything—EVERYTHING!"[54]

There are times in our lives when we become aware of our smallness and God's overwhelming greatness. His magnificence is not the kind that pulls us down so He can be exalted at our expense. Rather, His majesty motivates and calls us to higher standards and inspires us to serve noble purposes.

This afternoon when you sit quietly with your tea, ponder the greatness of God, the beautiful sacrifice of His Son Jesus, and the gentle power of His Holy Spirit within you. Let Him be Everything to you!

―――――――――――――

To the frightened, God is friendly; to the
poor in spirit, he is forgiving; to the
ignorant, considerate; to the weak, gentle;
to the stranger, hospitable.

A. W. TOZER

THE SPINNING WHEEL

In *Ordering Your Private World*, Gordon MacDonald tells the story of Mohandas Gandhi, the Hindu leader who was known as "India's George Washington" because he led his people to national independence. People who have read biographies of Gandhi or have seen his life portrayed in film are often impressed by his calm and serene character.

> Don't let the world around you squeeze you into its own mold.
>
> ROMANS 12:2
> PHILLIPS

Gandhi frequently was found among the poor and diseased in India's cities. He would walk among them offering a touch of hope, a word of encouragement, or a gentle affirming smile. The next day Gandhi might be found in palaces and government buildings negotiating with the most powerful and educated people of his age.

How did he keep a balanced sense of self in these vast extremes of Indian society? How did he maintain humility when the great masses of people cheered him as a hero or when he was summoned to talk with kings and government leaders?

Gandhi spun the wool from which his clothes were made. When he returned to his simple dwelling, he sat on the floor to spin wool on his spinning wheel. This simple chore restored to him a sense of who he was and what was basic, practical, and essential to life. It helped him to resist the public acclaim that might distort who he knew himself to be or distract him from the purpose he believed was his destiny.[55]

We each need to make an intentional effort in our lives to remain true to our deepest selves, that part of us which is created in God's image and designed to bring Him glory. Often we structure our lives around the activities in which we participate. But the Lord calls us to order our lives around His priorities and purposes. Then we can be His people in the world, but not of the world.

We are shaped and fashioned by what we love.

JOHANN WOLFGANG VON GOETHE

A SIP AT A TIME

The great movie maker Cecil B. DeMille once remarked on the importance of happiness in one's life and how to savor it:

> *The profession one chooses to follow for a livelihood seldom brings fame and fortune, but a life lived within the dictates of one's conscience can bring happiness and satisfaction of living far beyond worldly acclaim. I expect to pass through this world but once, and any good therefore that I can do, or any kindness that I can show to any fellow creature, let me do it now. Let me not defer or neglect it, for I shall not pass this way again. Happiness must be sipped, not drained from life in great gulps — nor does it flow in a steady stream like water from a faucet. "A portion of thyself" is a sip of happiness as satisfying as it is costless.[56]*

DeMille's slow-sipping metaphor reminds us that one may sit for quite some time with a mug of hot tea resting warmly between one's hands. The warm, fragrant steam helps to revive one's attitude and generally gives a feeling of contentment. In those moments, it is easier to agree with Paul: "I have learned in whatever state I am, to be content" (Philippians 4:11 NKJV).

My servants will sing out of the joy of their hearts.

ISAIAH 65:14

One of the ways in which we may experience true happiness is to "sip" from the supply of talents and abilities God gives us and use them to benefit others. "Sipping" doesn't require spending great amounts of time. Neither does it require extraordinary or professional helping skills.

Use a gift or talent you have to serve others. Volunteer for a committee at work, teach Sunday school, join a choir or musical group, coach little league, teach adults to read, or simply make an effort to get better acquainted with your colleagues.

Helen Keller, blind and deaf from the age of nineteen months, had remarkable sight when it came to viewing life's priorities. She said, "Many persons have a wrong idea about what constitutes true happiness. It is not attained through self-gratification, but through fidelity to a worthy purpose."

How miraculous it is that God has built an automatic measure of happiness into every act of self-sacrifice! Take a sip of happiness by serving others!

God can do tremendous things through
people who don't care who gets the credit.

UNKNOWN

KNOW YOUR OBJECTIVE

In the book *Work and Contemplation*, Douglas Steere tells a story from the Great Depression era when work was scarce, but people took great pride in whatever job they did. Instead of receiving welfare checks, able-bodied people were given what sometimes amounted to busywork in order to earn their pay. The program was created to add a measure of dignity to "being on the dole." Folks who did not have to take advantage of the program openly scorned it, while the workers who did join the program were often embarrassed they had to do so. Steere writes:

> The man who plants and the man who waters have one purpose, and each will be rewarded according to his own labor.
>
> 1 CORINTHIANS 3:8

> *Some years ago I heard the labor expert, Whiting Williams, tell of a squad of day laborers who were hired one morning and put to work. . . . The foreman . . . set them to digging holes some three feet deep. When a hole was finished, it was inspected and the workman was ordered to fill it up and come to another point and to dig another hole of the same depth.*

> *This went on for most of the morning and finally the foreman noted the group talking in a huddle and then their spokesman came to him and said . . . "We're gonna quit . . . give us our money. You ain't gonna make fools out of us!"*

The foreman's eyes narrowed, and then understanding broke over him, and he said quietly, "Can't you see, we're trying to find where the pipe is broken?"

"Oh," said the man, and after a hurried word with the others . . . returned and said, "Where do you want us to dig next?" [57]

Christians are frequently admonished to value one another's work and to work in a spirit of cooperation. This is easier when every member of the team clearly understands the objective. When the objective is finally attained, each is able to share in the satisfaction of seeing his or her contribution to the overall success.

Focus on the objectives you are working toward, and make certain the whole team has a clear understanding of the goals that have been set.

More men fail through lack of purpose than through lack of talent.

BILLY SUNDAY

CUT LOOSE!

An old farmer in northern India brought his goods to sell at the village bazaar. Among the items was a whole covey of quail. In order to keep them together, he tied a string around one leg of each bird and attached the strings to a ring which fit over a stick driven into the ground. The farmer exercised the birds by training them to walk around and around in a circle.

> Live as free men, yet without using your freedom as a pretext for evil; but live as servants of God.
>
> 1 PETER 2:16
> RSV

For most of the day, the farmer had no offers on the quail. Then along came a devout religious man of the highest Hindu caste. He had great reverence for all of life and felt deep, profound compassion for the little birds walking in a never-ending circle.

The religious man asked the farmer the price of the quail and then offered to buy them all. The farmer was elated. As the holy man handed him the money, however, the farmer was startled to hear him say, "Now, please, set them all free."

"What did you say?" the farmer asked.

The holy man repeated himself, saying, "You heard me. Cut the strings from their legs and turn them loose. Set them all free!"

Without another word, the farmer did as he was told. After all, the birds were no longer his—he had been compensated for them. Now what do you think the quail did? They continued their circular march around the center pole. When the religious man attempted to shoo them away, they landed not too far away and resumed their march.

Old habits and thought patterns can keep us from being who God wants us to be and from doing what He wants us to do. To be set free, there are times we must give ourselves a gentle push, and other times we must receive a nudge from someone else. One thing is certain, God desires us to live in freedom—a freedom Jesus purchased for us by way of the Cross and Resurrection.

There are two freedoms: the false, where man is free to do what he likes; the true, where a man is free to do what he ought.

CHARLES KINGSLEY

THE PLASTER SOLUTION

Disagreements are a natural part of working together—and different points of view are critical to creative and problem-solving processes. Still, the friction caused when differing opinions arise can cause needless pain and waste valuable time and energy. Occasionally, the best way to convince someone of your point of view while maintaining clear lines of communication is just to keep quiet and "start plastering."

Benjamin Franklin learned that plaster sown in the fields would make things grow. He told his neighbors, but they did not believe him, arguing that plaster could be of no use at all to grass or grain.

> A man hath joy by the answer of his mouth; and a word spoken in due season, how good is it!
>
> PROVERBS 15:23 KJV

After a little while, he allowed the matter to drop. But he went into the field early the next spring and sowed some grain. Close by the path, where people would walk, he traced some letters with his finger and put plaster into them.

After a week or two, the seed sprang up. His neighbors, as they passed that way, gasped at what they saw. Brighter green than all the rest of the field, sproutedFranklin's seeded message in large letters, "This has been plastered."

Benjamin Franklin did not need to argue with his

neighbors about the benefit of plaster any longer!

The answer to some disagreements may be to stop talking and try out several solutions together, measure them against like standards, and then resume the selection process. Meanwhile, tempers cool, objectivity returns, and new options can surface.

The best way to keep people from
jumping down your throat is to keep your
mouth shut.

UNKNOWN

TEA-TIME MANNERS

How much sweeter everyday life would be if tea-time manners were valued! Tea-time manners are more than waving a pinkie in the air, knowing which fork to use, or remembering where to place one's napkin after a meal. These are secondary to the real reason we have manners.

> The desire of a man is his kindness.
>
> PROVERBS 19:22 KJV

Manners are merely behaving as though Jesus were our honored Guest—as if every other person we meet were His personal emissary. It means doing and saying what makes others feel comfortable.

Some years ago, the members of an entire church in Scotland were able to produce one of the most remarkable preachers of the time just by showing him Christlike manners. Here's what happened:

Ian Maclaren, author of Beside the Bonnie Brier Bush, was learning to preach without notes at his first church assignment in the Highlands. At times, he would stop in the middle of a sermon and say to the congregation, "Friends, that is not very clear. It was clear in my study on Saturday, but now I will begin again."

After one particular service when his memory had failed him, Maclaren was approached by a gaunt elder who took him by the hand and said, "When you are not remembering your sermon, just call out a psalm, and we will be singing that while you are taking a rest; for we all are loving you and praying for you."

With such parishioners, how could Ian Maclaren have done anything other than grow in his preaching abilities and pulpit composure? That first Highland church made Ian Maclaren. Years later he said, "I am in the ministry today because of those country folk, those perfect gentlemen and Christians."

If one has developed a sense of manners, then he or she is less likely to have to stop and say, "What would Jesus do in this situation?"

—————————

Little drops of water, little grains of sand, make the mighty ocean and the pleasant land. Little deeds of kindness, little words of love, help to make Earth happy like the heaven above.

JULIA A. FLETCHER CARNEY

STEP RIGHT UP

"Getting away from it all" takes on a whole new meaning when you decide, as a young Scottish girl did, to walk around the world. A troubled home life convinced her she needed a change of scenery, as well as a challenge that would test her mettle.

How does one go about walking around the world? In Ffyona's case, she spent eleven years and covered more than nineteen thousand miles walking from northern Scotland to southern England; New York to Los Angeles; Sydney to Perth, Australia; and South Africa to Morocco. Along the way, she fought disease, poisonous insects, bad weather, blisters, stonings, and loneliness.

Blessed are those who hear the joyful blast of the trumpet, for they shall walk in the light of your presence.

PSALM 89:15
TLB

To keep herself going, she had to come up with a way to motivate her often tired feet. She quickly discovered that if she could focus her mind on doing what had to be done to make it through each phase of the walk, her body would do the rest. The stronger her mind, the better her body performed. Another of Ffyona's important discoveries was that she needed to take one day at a time. Each day she would say to herself, "If I walk ten miles right now, I can stop and have a meal." Building in breaks and small rewards along the way made it much easier for her to stay committed to her bigger goal.[58]

Walking seems like such a simple thing to do. But, oh, the power of a walk! Even when we have no particular destination, our feet can take us to a new place and give us both a physical and a psychological break from where we've been. Walking away from a heated debate is sometimes the smartest thing to do and the best way to protect a relationship. Crossing a room to talk to someone who looks lonely is often the first step in building a new friendship.

The steps of good men are directed by
the Lord.

PSALM 37:23 TLB

When we are obedient, God guides our
steps and our stops.

CORRIE TEN BOOM

HALT!

Those who counsel the clinically depressed often suggest the HALT! Method to their patients. HALT is an acronym based upon these four words:

- Hungry
- Angry
- Lonely
- Tired

Too much of any of these conditions can result in a stress overload and lead to a downward spiral that eventually crashes into a form of depression. When two or more of these conditions are present, the downward plunge happens faster, with greater pain. And, if all four conditions are present as an ongoing pattern in a person's life, the person's depression may not only be deep, but life itself may be endangered.

To compound the problem, hunger, anger, loneliness, and exhaustion tend to cluster together. If you are overly tired, it's easier to become angry. If you have missed a meal, you are likely to get tired more quickly, and so forth.

Let us strip off anything that slows us down or holds us back, and especially those sins that wrap themselves so tightly around our feet and trip us up.

HEBREWS 12:1 TLB

Therefore, any time you are feeling too hungry, too angry, too lonely, or too tired . . . it's time to call a HALT! and to take immediate remedial action. Have a healthy bite to eat. Release your anger in prayer, exercise, or an act of reconciliation. Call a friend, and pour out your heart. Take a nap, or go to bed early.

"Call it to a halt" and "enough is enough" are well-known phrases we need to apply on a daily basis. Don't neglect your personal nutrition. Get enough sleep. Balance your life with friendships. Live in peace with the people around you.

As you prepare to come to the end of your workday, it's especially important you remember to HALT! Don't push yourself into overdrive, even if you have to work overtime. Avoid setting yourself up for a crash by staying well fed, calm, in touch with friends, and refreshed.

"Holy leisure" refers to a sense of balance
in the life, an ability to be at peace
through the actives of the day, an ability
to rest and take time to enjoy beauty, and
ability to pace ourselves.

RICHARD FOSTER

SWEET REVENGE?

A young and hot-tempered officer in the army struck a foot soldier. The foot soldier was noted for his courage. He felt the insult deeply, but military discipline forbade him to return the blow. He said with conviction, however, "I will make you repent it."

> If thine enemy hunger, feed him; if he thirst, give him drink; for in so doing thou shalt heap coals of fire on his head. Be not overcome of evil, but overcome evil with good.
>
> ROMANS 12:20-21 KJV

One day in the heat of battle the foot soldier saw an officer who was wounded and separated from his company. He gallantly forced his way through enemy lines to the officer, whom he recognized as the one who had insulted him. Nevertheless, he supported the wounded man with one arm as the two fought their way back to their own lines.

Trembling with emotion, the officer grasped the hand of the soldier and stammered out his gratitude, "Noble man! What a return for an insult so carelessly given!"

The young man pressed his hand in turn and with a smile said gently, "I told you I would make you repent it." From that time on they were as brothers.

John Wesley found another positive and helpful way to settle quarrels. In his journal he wrote of a disagreement that took place in one of the religious gatherings called Societies. Fourteen people were expelled from the group as a result. Not seeing any good reason why such an action should have taken place, Wesley called the entire group together to try to bring about reconciliation.

Prior to the sermon, prayer, and communion, Wesley recalls, "I willingly received them all again; requiring only one condition of the contenders on both sides, to say not one word of anything that was past." Fie then goes on to describe the healing that took place in the group when the recounting of old wounds was eliminated as a possibility.

Extending God's grace to those who have wronged us can repair just about any broken relationship. Instead of returning anger with anger, choose to use kindness.

By taking revenge, a man is but even with his enemy; but in passing over it, he is superior.

FRANCIS BACON

MISSED MANNERS

> Before honor
> is humility.
>
> PROVERBS 15:33
> KJV

During the Coolidge Administration, an overnight guest at the White House found himself in a terribly embarrassing predicament. At the family breakfast table he was seated at the president's right hand. To his surprise he saw Coolidge take his coffee cup, pour the greater portion of its contents into the deep saucer, and leisurely add a little bit of cream and sugar.

The guest was so disconcerted he lost his head. With a panicky feeling that it was incumbent upon him to do as the president did, he hastily poured his own coffee into his saucer. But he froze with horror as he watched Coolidge place his own saucer on the floor for the cat![59]

We may never have been guests at the White House, but we uncomfortable situations where we were unsure of ourselves and the proper etiquette for the occasion. Scripture describes the proper protocol for entering the presence of God. The psalmist tells us, "Enter into His gates with thanksgiving, And into His courts with praise" (Psalm 100:4 NKJV). We go into the Lord's presence with gratitude and joy for all He is and does in our lives.

King David asked, "Who may ascend into the hill of the Lord? Or who may stand in His holy place?" and then answered, "He who has clean hands and a pure heart, Who has not lifted up his soul to an idol, Nor sworn deceitfully" (Psalm 24:3-4 NKJV).

The writer of the Book of Hebrews said that Jesus made a way to God for us. We can approach His throne with confidence and "receive mercy and find grace to help us in our time of need" (Hebrews 4:16).

We don't have to worry about how we come to the Lord when we approach with pure and expectant hearts, understanding that before honor comes humility.

Christ is not one of many ways to approach God, nor is he the best of several ways; he is the only way.

A. W. TOZER

COUNT ON IT!

Tea is the second-largest consumer beverage in the world—ranking only behind water. Its origins reach back four thousand years in time. The story goes that one day the Chinese Emperor Shen Nung knelt before a fire while he was boiling water. The wise emperor was called the "Divine Healer," and he always boiled water before drinking it. Nobody knew the causes of illnesses, but Shen Nung had observed that people who boiled their drinking water had better health.

> Jesus Christ is the same yesterday and today and forever.
>
> HEBREWS 13:8
> RSV

Shen Nung's servants had made a fire from the branch of a nearby tree. As the water began to boil, some of the topmost leaves of the branches were blown into the pot of water.

The emperor exclaimed, "What a delightful aroma!" as the fragrance of tea floated into the air for the first time. He then sipped the aromatic steaming liquid. "Ah!" he said, "What a flavor!" And that is how tea was discovered in China in the year 2737 B.C. Tea is now consumed in every nation of the world.[60]

Society today places great value on newness. Seminars, workshops, and conferences abound, each offering new methods and formulas to achieve success. Stores advertise new styles of shoes, clothing, wallpaper, furniture, and electronics. If it's new, it's good! But is newness always the best?

Two thousand years ago Jesus said, "I am the way, the truth, and the life" (John 14:6 NKJV), and His Word is true today. You can count on it, no matter what new ideas you encounter in the world. As you sip your tea — just as people have for centuries — remind yourself that God's Word stands the test of time and serves as your foundation in every situation.

I'll trust in God's unchanging word till

soul and body sever; for though all things

hall pass away, his word shall stand

forever!

MARTIN LUTHER

ACCESSIBILITY

The end of a workday is a time when you may find it very pleasant and beneficial to make yourself a little more accessible to other people.

If you have had a "closed-door, nose-to-the-grindstone" attitude all day, now may be the time to open the door. If you've been on the phone for what seems like hours, now may be the time to wander the halls and have a brief face-to-face conversation with a colleague or someone you supervise.

> A man who has friends must himself be friendly.
>
> PROVERBS 18:24
> NKJV

If you have felt bogged down with paperwork or glued to a computer screen, now may be the time to walk to the cafeteria and get an energizing snack. Invite someone to go with you or meet you there for a few moments of casual conversation. If you have been indoors with children or house chores, it might be time to call a neighborhood friend and go for a walk.

Robert Fulghum has written: "The grass is not, in fact, always greener on the other side of the fence. Fences have nothing to do with it. The grass is greenest where it is watered."

Every day, regardless of our environment or situation, we need to have human contact and communication. God built this need into us, and from the story of God's relationship with Adam and Eve in the Garden of Eden, we can assume that God enjoyed a late-in-the-day stroll with His creation—a time of sharing lives, not simply working together on tasks.

Share with others in a heart-to-heart way. Listen with open ears to the feelings people may be expressing, even more closely than you listen to the details of their story. Be willing to help carry their burdens and rejoice at their victories. Allow yourself to be vulnerable to others in return—revealing your own wounds, concerns, worries, frustrations, hopes, dreams, and desires. Accessibility is the first key to a genuine relationship.

No man is an island. Entire of himself;
every man is a piece of a continent, a part
of the main.

JOHN DONNE

COPING SKILLS

How we handle delays tells us a lot about ourselves. How do you handle a traffic jam when you left the house already late for work? What do you do when your flight is delayed because of mechanical difficulty or bad weather? How do you respond when the register in your checkout lane runs out of tape just as you get to the head of the line? Can you take a deep breath and enjoy a five-minute break at the railroad crossing when the guard rail goes down to allow a train to pass?

Consider how one man handled a delay. Just as the light turned green at the busy intersection, his car stalled in heavy traffic. He tried everything he knew to get the car started again, but all his efforts failed. The chorus of honking behind him put him on edge, which only made matters worse.

Finally he got out of his car and walked back to the first driver and said, "I'm sorry, but I can't seem to get my car started. If you'll go up there and give it a try, I'll stay here and blow your horn for you."

> My times are in your hand.
>
> PSALM 31:15
> NRSV

Things rarely go as smoothly as we would like, and we don't usually schedule ourselves any extra time just in case something goes wrong.

The ability to accept disappointments, delays, and setbacks with a pleasant, generous spirit is a gift of graciousness that comes from one who has received grace from others in pressured circumstances. Life is a series of choices, and no matter what situation we are in, we always have the freedom to choose how we are going to respond.

Refuse to get out of sorts the next time your schedule gets interrupted or turned upside down. Pray for strength to remain calm, cheerful, relaxed, and refreshed in the midst of the crisis. And always remember: God's plans for you are not thwarted by delays!

Never become irritable while waiting; if you are patient, you'll find that you can wait much faster.

UNKNOWN

OPPOSITES BALANCED

Much of life seems to be suspended between opposites. We grow up learning to label things as good or bad, hurtful or helpful, naughty or nice. People are kind or mean. The thermostat can be adjusted to avoid extremes of heat and cold. We look forward to the changing of seasons from summer to winter. Time is divided by day and night.

Not only are these opposites helpful to us in defining or "bordering" our lives, but they can help us release stress as well.

Very often people who are engaged in physical, muscle-intensive work all day choose a mental activity with which to relax and unwind. Those who have idea-intensive jobs often enjoy relaxing with hobbies that make use of their hands, such as woodcarving or needlework. Those in sterile, well-ordered environments look forward to going home to weed their gardens.

Structured tasks and routines are good relaxation for those involved in the creative arts. The musician runs home to the computer. The surgeon delights in

The day is yours, the night also is yours; you have prepared the light and the sun. You have set all the borders of the Earth; you have made summer and winter.

PSALMS 74:16-17 NKJV

growing orchids in a hothouse. The factory worker enjoys crossword puzzles. The executive unwinds in the kitchen, preparing gourmet meals.

The Lord created us for this rhythm of opposites. God told Noah as he and his family left the ark that Noah would experience "Seedtime and harvest, And cold and heat, And winter and summer, And day and night Shall not cease" (Genesis 8:22 NKJV). Human beings were set in a world of opposites.

When you feel stressed out at day's end, try engaging in an activity that is opposite in nature to the work you have been doing. If you have been using your mind, turn to an activity that is physical. If you have been exerting physical energy, turn to an activity that is mental.

Let the pendulum swing back to rest in a central location.

Renewal and restoration are not luxuries.
They are essentials.

CHARLES R. SWINDOLL

A FIRM FOUNDATION

The world's tallest tower stands in Toronto, Ontario, Canada. The first observation deck rises to 1,136 feet, and the second is even higher at 1,815 feet. Photographs and information located inside the tower help visitors comprehend the enormous undertaking of the project. Sixty-two tons of earth and shale were removed from fifty feet into the ground for laying the concrete that rises to the sky.

> The rain came down, the streams rose, and the winds blew and beat against that house yet it did not fall, because it had its foundation on the rock.
>
> MATTHEW 7:25

From 1972 to 1974, 3,000 workers were at the tower site. Harnessed by safety ropes, some of the laborers dangled outside the giant for their finishing work. Remarkably, no one sustained injuries nor died on location. Today a rapid elevator transports visitors upward for a breathtaking view of the city and all surrounding areas. Many feel it was well worth the money, time, and effort required to build the CN Tower.

We, too, need a good foundation for facing life each day. As we pray and spend time with our Heavenly Father, we are strengthening our spiritual foundation, our support base for life. We are able to see more from His point of view and not just our own. Thus we are not overwhelmed by whatever comes our way. When we feel we're hanging on the edge or suspended in mid-air, we can take courage in knowing He is holding us — firmly planted — in the palm of His hand. His foundation is strong and sure, and He will not crumble and fall.

Faith is the christian's foundation, hope is
his anchor, death is his harbor, Christ is
his pilot, and heaven is his country.

JEREMY TAYLOR

TIME FOR A CHANGE

Skier Jean-Claude Killy was ready to do whatever it took—no matter how hard the work—to be the best when he made the French national team in the early 1960s. But after months of grueling practice, he recognized that his competitors were putting in just as much effort in the same kind of training. It was then he decided to go a step further and find different ways to ski faster rather than just working harder.

> Now faith is the assurance of things hoped for, the conviction of things not seen.
>
> HEBREWS 11:1 NASB

He started testing every part of his racing technique, such as altering the accepted leg positions and using his poles in unorthodox ways. Soon, his experiments resulted in an explosive new style that cut his racing times dramatically. Within a few years, Killy won virtually every major skiing trophy and three gold medals in the 1968 Winter Olympics.[61]

Killy learned an important lesson in creativity: Innovations don't require genius—just a willingness to question the norms and try something different.

It's been said that one reason people eventually stop growing and learning is they become less willing to risk failure by trying new ideas or experiences. Change can be difficult and uncomfortable. But if our ambitions are only to avoid the discomforts of life, we could soon find we have very little life at all.

God wants us to have the most joyful, fulfilling life possible, and sometimes that requires stepping out into the unknown. Is there a new experience or idea you've been hesitant to pursue? You'll never know until you try.

Be satisfied with nothing but your best.

EDWARD ROWLAND SILL

I CAN SEE
CLEARLY NOW

Between Macon and Valdosta, Georgia, lies a stretch of Interstate 75, known for heavy fog that causes massive pileups of cars, vans, trucks, and campers. Several times each year horrible accidents happen as drivers enter the thick fog. Many can't even see the front of their own vehicles, much less beyond.

> We know that, when he appears we shall be like him, because we shall see him just as he is.
>
> 1 JOHN 3:2
> NASB

The result is a disaster waiting to happen—and often it does. Many people are injured, vehicles are destroyed, and motorists are delayed for hours. The costs to personal property and the city and state, as well as the increase in insurance rates are astronomical. But the worst tragedy is the loss of human life.

Drivers involved in these accidents will tell you the same story. They saw the fog but didn't think it was as thick as it turned out to be. They hoped to pass through it safely by turning their blinkers on and driving slowly. These drivers had no idea that many vehicles in front of them had already been forced to stop—often victims of whatever tragedy had occurred to a car or truck ahead of them.

In this life, we may see things through a fog of confusion or circumstances. But the day will come when we can stand before Christ, when we will see Him clearly just as He is, in all His glory. Nothing will be able to cloud the true and living Christ from our vision when we go to Heaven.

The good news is that we don't have to wait. Today, right now, we can see Him clearly through His Word and in the lives of our Godly brothers and sisters.

Heaven is the place where questions and answers become one.

ELIE WIESEL

REFERNCES

ENDNOTES

1. Reader's Digest (March 1991) pp. 128-132.

2. A Guide to Prayer for All God's People, Rueben P. Job and Norman Shawchuck, eds. (Nashville: Upper Room Books, pp. 255-256.

3. Encyclopedia Judaica, Prof. Cecil Roth and Dr. Geoffrey Wigoder, eds. (Jerusalem: Kefer Publishing House, 1972) Vol. 4, pp. 142-143.

4. Doris Donnelly, Spiritual Fitness (San Francisco: Harper, 1993) pp. 111-124.

5. "Leisure," The Family Book of Best Loved Poems, David L. George, ed. (Garden City, NY: Doubleday & Co., 1952) p. 261.

6. The Treasure Chest, Brian Culhane, ed. (San Francisco: Harper, 1995) p. 162.

7. Craig B. Larson, Illustrations for Preaching & Teaching (Grand Rapids, MI: Baker Book House, 1993) p. 190.

8. Treasury of the Christian Faith, Stanley Stuber and Thomas Clark, eds. (NY: Association Press, 1949) p. 355.

9. The Treasure Chest, Brian Culhane, ed. (San Francisco: Harper, 1995) p. 171.

10. Ibid.

11. Lloyd John Ogilvie, Silent Strength for My Life (Eugene, OR: Harvest House Publishers, 1990) p. 113.

12. Walter B. Knight, Knight's Master Book of 4,000 Illustrations (Grand Rapids, MI: William B. Eerdmans Publishing Co., 1956) p. 615.

13. JAMA (January 10, 1996) p. 99.

14. Arden Autry.

15. Daily Bread (July 20, 1992).

16. George Sweeting, Who Said That? (Chicago, IL: Moody Press, 1995).

17. Newsweek (February 15, 1999) p.47.

18. Jim Gleason (Transplant Recipient Support List: trnsplnt@wuvmd.wustl edu).

19. Today in the "Word (February 1991) p. 10.

20. Barbara Hatcher, Vital Speeches (March 1, 1987).

21. Today in the Word, Moody Bible Institute (January 1992) p. 8.

22. Swindoll, Hand Me Another Brick (Thomas Nelson, 1978) pp. 82, 88.

23. Ibid.

24. Ansel Adams, Morning Edition 11-24-97 (National Public Radio).

25. Paul Meier, M.D., "Confessions of a Workaholic," The Physician (March/April 1990).

26. Author Unknown,"Opportunities Missed."

27. George Sweeting, Who Said That? (Moody Press, Chicago, IL.1995).

28. Today in the Word (September 25, 1992).

29. Joy Dickinson, "A Mixed Blessing," The Dallas Morning News (January 10, 1999).

30. Kenneth A. Brown, Inventors at Work: Interviews with 16 Notable American Inventors.

31. Leslie B. Flynn, Come Alive with Illustrations (Baker Book House, Grand Rapids, MI: 1988).

32. Greenville Herald Banner, "USA Weekend" (April 19, 1996).

33. David Mackenzie, Still Married, Still Sober (IVP, p. 117.

34. Paul Aurandt, Paul Harvey's The Rest of the Story (New York: Doubleday & Company, 1977).

35. Doris Donnelly, Spiritual Fitness (NY: Harper-SanFrancisco, A Division of HarperCollins, 1993) pp. 155-156, 165-166.

36. Jamie Buckingham, The Last Word (Plainfield, NJ: Logos International, 1978) pp. 169-170.

37. Kenneth W. Osbeck, 101 More Hymn Stories (Grand Rapids, MI: Kregel Publications, 1985) pp. 24-26.

38. Ron Rand,"Won by One," The Inspirational Study Bible, Max Lucado, ed. (Dallas: Word, 1995) pp. 604-605.

39. Denis Waitley and Reni L. Witt, The Joy of Working (NY: Dodd, Mead Sc Company, 1985) pp. 213-214.

40. Songs of My Soul: Devotional Thoughts from the Writings of W. Phillip Keller, A1 Bryant, ed. (Dallas: Word, 1989) p. 77.

41. Jim Stovall, You Don't Have to Be Blind to See (Nashville, TN: Thomas Nelson Publishers, 1996) p. 90.

42. John Baillie, A Diary of Readings (NY: Collier Books, Macmillan Publishing Co., 1955) Day 202.

43. Creative Living (Autumn 1995) pp. 20-24.

44. Kenneth W. Osbeck, Amazing Grace (Grand Rapids, MI: Kregel Publications, 1993) p. 228.

45. The Treasure Chest, Brian Culhane, ed. (San Francisco: HarperCollins 1995) p. 10.

46. Rabbi Joseph Telushkin, Jewish Wisdom (NY: William Morrow and Company, Inc., 1994) pp. 182-184.

47. The World's Best Religious Quotations, James Gilchrist Lawson, ed. (NY: Fleming H. Revell Company, 1930) p. 99.

48. John Baillie, A Diary of Readings (Collier Books, Macmillan Publishing Co., NY, 1955) Day 182.

49. People (March 18, 1996) p. 62.

50. James S. Hewett, Illustrations Unlimited (Wheaton, IL: Tyndale House, 1988) pp. 410-411.

51. Lewis Smedes, Forgive and Forget: Healing the Hurts We Don't Deserve (NY: Harper & Row, 1984) pp. 86-89.

52. San Luis ObispoTelegram/Tribune (March 16, 1996) p. E4.

53. Paul Lee Tan, Encyclopedia of 7700 Illustrations (Garland, TX: Bible Communications Inc., 1979) pp. 1477-1479.

54. Daily Readings from the Works of Leslie D. Weatherhead, Frank Cumbers, ed. (Nashville: Abingdon Press, 1968) p. 285.

55. Gordon MacDonald, Ordering Your Private World (Nashville: Oliver-Nelson, 1984, 1985) p. 177.

56. E. Paul Hovey, The Treasury of Inspirational Anecdotes, Quotations & Illustrations (Grand Rapids, MI: Fleming H. Revell (Baker Books), 1994) pp. 204-205.

57. Ibid., p. 223.

58. Health (March/April 1995) pp. 48-49.

59. Thesaurus of Anecdotes, Edmund Fuller, ed. (NY: The Wise Book Co., 1945) p. 103.

60. Aubrey Franklin, Teatime by the Tea Ambassador (NY: Frederick Fell Publishers, Inc., 1981) pp. 4-5.

61. Readers Digest, October 1991, p. 61.